PRIVATE LESSONS
NOTICING THAT GOD NOTICES YOU
PRIVATE BATTLES
Every day, Everywhere, Every moment

•••

DAISY JONES

Private Lessons. Private Battles. Noticing that God Notices You
Every day, Everywhere, Every moment

Copyright © 2022 Daisy Jones
All Rights Reserved.

ISBN 979-8-9865071-2-5

In accordance with international copyright laws, scanning, uploading, reproducing, storing in an electronic system, or transmitted in any form or by any means, electronic, mechanical, photocopy, recording, or otherwise without prior written permission from the author constitutes unlawful piracy and theft of the author's intellectual property. Brief quotations may be used in a literary review.

P.O. Box 1407
Hinesville, Georgia 31310
www.conversationswithdaisyjones.com

Although every precaution has been taken to verify the accuracy of the information contained herein, the author and publisher assume no responsibility for any errors or omissions. No liability is assumed for any liability, loss, or risk, personal or otherwise, which is incurred as a consequence, directly or indirectly, of the use and application of any of the contents of this book.

Scripture quotations marked "NLT" are taken from the Holy Bible, New Living Translation, copyright © 1996, 2004, 2007 by Tyndale House Foundation. Used by permission of Tyndale House Publishers, Inc., Carol Stream, Illinois 60188.

Scripture quotations marked "MSG" or "The Message" are taken from The Message. Copyright © 1993, 1994, 1995, 1996, 2000, 2001, 2002. Used by permission of NavPress Publishing Group.

Scripture quotations marked "AMP" are taken from the Amplified® Bible. Copyright © 1954, 1958, 1962, 1964, 1965, 1987 by The Lockman Foundation. Used by permission.

Scripture quotations marked "NKJV" are taken from the New King James Version. Copyright © 1982 by Thomas Nelson, Inc. Used by permission.

Scripture quotations marked "ESV" are from the ESV Bible® (The Holy Bible, English Standard Version®). Copyright © 2001 by Crossway Bibles, a publishing ministry of Good News Publishers. Used by permission. All rights reserved.

Scripture quotations marked "KJV" are taken from the Holy Bible, King James Version in the public domain.

Scripture quotations marked "NIV" are taken from the Holy Bible, New International Version®, NIV®. Copyright © 1973, 1978, 1984, 2011 by Biblica, Inc.™ Used by permission of Zondervan. All rights reserved worldwide. www.zondervan.com. The "NIV" and "New International Version" are trademarks registered in the United States Patent and Trademark Office by Biblica, Inc.™

Cover Design:
Daisy Jones

Interior Layout & Design and Cover Layout:
Tarsha L. Campbell

Published by:
DOMINIONHOUSE
Publishing & Design, LLC
P.O. Box 681938 | Orlando, Florida 32868
407.703.4800 phone | www.mydominionhouse.com

DEDICATION

*To those who are open to a deeper connection
with and consciousness of God
on this unpredictable, joyous, and
often chaotic journey of life*

"Write everything I tell
you in a book."
Jeremiah 30:2

REMEMBERING

Teal
Dad
Professor Hines

CONTENTS

Foreword
Introduction

PART I
The Power of Noticing

One	**Quiet Loudness**	
	God Is Still Speaking 21	
Two	**Origins**	
	From Where?. 33	
Three	**Private Practice**	
	No Degree Required 47	
Four	**The Power of Noticing**	
	Did You See That?. 71	
Five	**Six Notes of Denial**	
	No More Missed Moments. 79	
Six	**What to Do When the Problem Is You**	
	Say Less. 93	
Seven	**Battle-Tested Lessons**	
	Experienced, Toughened, Seasoned 111	

CONTENTS

PART II
God Notices Us

Eight   **Moses: Quiet Loudness**
God Is Still Speaking 127

Nine   **Devotion: Private Practice**
Undeniable Results 131

Ten   **Jacob: The Power of Noticing**
Alone Time 135

Eleven   **David: When the Problem Is You**
Own It 139

Twelve   **Thinking About It**
Words to Live By 145

ACKNOWLEDGMENTS 153

ABOUT THE AUTHOR 154

CONTACT THE AUTHOR 155

"God has given Daisy a unique and much-needed perspective in these dire times. She gives us permission to be ourselves and become more aware of God's presence by noticing the inner promptings during our best times and our worst times."

FOREWORD

I am one of Daisy's oldest and best friends. We met in the military almost twenty-five years ago. Throughout our friendship, we have shared our love for God and his Word. We've talked about knowing God, following God, understanding God, and serving God by serving others. We've sat for hours discussing God's infinite love, power, and grace, and encouraged each other in the faith.

When Daisy told me she was writing a book, I thought, "It's about time." She has a propensity to climb high mountains, and some might say she is an overachiever. But the truth is, Daisy is multi-talented, driven, and brings a spirit of excellence to everything she does.

I am extremely excited that she completed this book. I know God has poured into her and her life experiences qualify her to write *Private Lessons. Private Battles.*

God has given Daisy a unique and much-needed perspective in these dire times. She gives us permission to be ourselves and become more aware of God's presence by noticing the inner promptings during our best times and our worst times. She creates a refreshing path for those who feel abandoned, distant, broken, invisible, and discouraged. She signals agreement with those who have wondered if God sees them, hears them, feels them, and will attend to them. She helps us to recognize that indeed God does.

This book must be read again and again. It will challenge you, encourage you, and empower you. It is a jarring experience that you will love.

Congratulations, Daisy, for your masterful work. Through your labor of love, we are reminded of what matters. The more sinful the world becomes, the more silent God seems to be. *Private Lessons. Private Battles* reminds us that God is never silent. He is Almighty God, and He speaks loudly–always.

K. E. Clark
Author, *Your Pathway to Abundant Living* and *Wholly Man*

"Then those who respected the Lord spoke to one another, and the Lord took notice. A book was prepared before Him in which were recorded the names of those who respected the Lord and honored His name."

—Malachi 3:16 NET

"...What I do think is that this book matters. It will help you live more fully and freely, as you open up to a deeper connection with and consciousness of God on this sometimes chaotic, confusing, overwhelming, and unpredictable journey."

INTRODUCTION

I FOUGHT TO GET HERE.

I have been a writer for as long as I can remember, always journaling, penning poetry, and writing songs.

When I was eleven years old, I wrote a letter to God about my hair. I burned a patch of it with my mother's hot comb. I didn't have permission to use the comb, nor did I know it would be too hot for my soft-textured hair until I saw the smoke, heard the frying, and smelled singed hair. It happened so quickly. I was horrified. I don't remember when, or how long afterward, but I wrote a letter asking God to let my hair grow back fast. I tucked the letter under my pillow. I don't remember if it was one day or days, but one of my younger brothers found the letter and told the rest of the family. I was embarrassed but kept silent through all the teasing about the letter—not my hair. They laughed and made fun of me. I never wrote a letter to God again.

I wrote poetry and later wrote for my college yearbook. When I was a second lieutenant, my battalion commander called me to his office one day; he wanted me to write weekly stories about the unit for the post newspaper.

Over fifteen years ago, I wrote for a local newspaper and won a Georgia Press Association award. I have written all kinds of things, but nothing like this, although my letter to God comes close.

PRIVATE LESSONS, PRIVATE BATTLES

When I first decided to write this book, back in 2005, it seemed doable. I had the title and the premise, and I began writing. It wasn't long before I had several chapters, but then I felt stuck. Within a year or two, getting to the finishing line seemed like a daunting task. Writer's block? No. It was fear. I can't talk about lessons without talking about battles. *Basically, I was not about to tell anyone private things, much less put them in a book.*

In 2016, my whole mindset changed. First, I couldn't shake the voice urging me to focus on "being" instead of "doing." I had to learn to not just slow down but stop, be quiet, listen, see, and think about what this book meant. Second, I had to recognize that I was defending a wrong mindset about life, worth, success, and relationships. Then it happened—in 2021, I finally grasped what had besieged my heart and mind for all those years.

> "There is no greater agony than bearing an untold story inside you."
>
> —Maya Angelou

And now, here we are!

This book has been the greatest challenge of my life. Someone said that the best writers write with honesty. That means I've had to voice my thoughts from an honest place, and this book is the result of it. It has been shaped, formulated, and distilled over time into what it is today. I've changed dramatically because of this book, and I've learned from it. You can't write a book like this and not change and learn from it. I needed this book and I believe you do too. This book is not a rant, a tell-all, or a confession of past mistakes, regrets, unspoken words, and unshed tears; it doesn't address any unresolved or unhealed hurts of the past. I no longer have any and I don't believe rehashing those things will benefit you or me. What I do think is that this book matters. It will help you live more fully and freely, as you open up to a deeper connection with and consciousness of God on this sometimes chaotic, confusing, overwhelming, and unpredictable journey.

I pray that it will help you be attentive to every moment in life, with an understanding that God is present, that He is intentionally and strategically speaking to you. He speaks with quiet loudness. Through his creation. Through life's private and personal battles. Through the mundane, the ordinary, and often the simple. Through triumphs. Through failures. Through highs and lows. Through wellness and illness. Through pain. Through regret. Through success. Through love. Through rejection. Through grief. Through a global pandemic.

Through it all—anywhere, any way, and any time He wants to.

God notices you. God sees you. God feels you. God hears you.

James 4:8–10, NKJV, tells us, "Draw near to God, and He will draw near to you." We have the honor, privilege, and choice to tune into His frequency to listen. We discover the depth, width, and height of His love and Presence as we tune in. One of the most powerful discoveries in life, is drawing near to God and His love—priceless and overflowing with inner strength.

Have you ever had tutoring sessions, private swimming lessons, music lessons, dance lessons, or specialized training sessions? Lessons focused on teaching you something new or reviewing something you already know? Lessons to increase your proficiency, talent, critical thinking, or any other skill? Private lessons invest in potential, *and they are not cheap*. Keep this in mind as you move through this book with me.

I have organized this book into two parts, with a total of twelve chapters—Part I: The Power of Noticing and Part II: God Notices You. I will challenge you with relevant questions and prompts at the end of each chapter in Part 1 to cultivate deeper thought and honest self-evaluation. In Part II, we will walk alongside individuals from the scriptures to further illuminate what we discussed in Part I.

I have tried my best to break down and unpack what I believe is timely and urgent. I started out trying to be formal, diplomatic, and conservative, but then I learned that saying something with diplomacy and formality doesn't work when you need to get the message across. So put it out there without fluff and apology. Just speak truthfully. Talk plainly. It works. That's what I've tried to do.

I want to help you understand and respond to God's vast and unconditional love, attentiveness, thoughts about you, and plans for you.

After reading this book, your life will change. Your view will change. You will have a fresh awareness of God, El Roi, and say He is "the God who sees me."

You will learn from it, as I have.

Thank you very much for choosing to read this book. I know this is so much bigger than you and I.

Take a deep breath. Let's dive in.

"We want big directional signs from God. God just wants us to pay attention."

-Lysa TerKeurst
Proverbs 31 Ministries

PART I
THE POWER OF NOTICING

...

"I bore witness to this quiet and
loud moment. It was a
holy moment. Isolated and
powerful. Unexpected and
powerful. It dawned on me, rather
it dropped on me in that sacred
moment that I was the only one
witnessing the last minutes
of this life..."

Quiet Loudness
God Is Still Speaking

CHAPTER ONE

"Awesome is loud, but awe is quiet."
—*Kevin McCloud, British designer*

I walked along the driveway that day like I would have on any other day. My husband, Nathan, was visiting our youngest grandsons in the next town, and I was home alone. I walked along the driveway about once per hour to get away from my desk and enjoy being outdoors, which I absolutely love. I can understand why God created Eden, that incredible and perfect garden. Beauty, splendor, and peace in one place. Eden was an ideal place of fulfillment visually, mentally, emotionally, and, of course, spiritually.

Genesis 2:8 NIV gives us this picture: "Then the LORD God planted a garden in Eden, in the east. He put the man he just made in it. GOD made all kinds of trees grow from the ground, trees beautiful to look at and good to eat." The entire historical account can be found in the Book of Genesis.

Can't you see and smell the blossoms, see the squirrels, hear the birds, see the ants and butterflies, see the leaves on the tall trees spanning the garden and providing shade and breeze? It was amazing. And the quiet stillness. The sounds of nature. The sounds of life. I can only imagine such perfection because even simply being outside is so soothing, almost therapeutic—at least when there are no mosquitoes or gnats. I live in southeast Georgia, so you can probably imagine the odds.

But I still love to take walks or sit alone to experience the quiet loudness and beauty of God's creation.

Two-hundred-and-forty-nine steps round-trip. I walked four more times around the driveway to achieve my step goal for the hour. There were no annoying gnats or flies buzzing and flitting around my ears, and the evening was absolutely beautiful.

QUIETNESS HAS A SOUND

It was strangely quiet. The sun was going down, but there was still daylight. There were no cars or trucks on the street, which made the evening feel even more serene. I noticed how quiet it was, and the quietness seemed loud. I know that's an oxymoron.

But it was so quiet that I could hear silence. I kept walking and noticed some movement in the distance, under an oak tree that stood ten feet or so to my right in the clearing. Looking from our front door, the clearing was to the left of the driveway, and walking back toward the house it was on my right. It had a few oak trees—none too big—and one or two very tall pine trees. I slowed and then stopped walking entirely, scanning the area to see what was going on. I have to admit that, usually, any slight movement will cause my sixty-year-old body to break into a full-blown sprint. Seriously. Tell me we can't move when we need to!

But I wasn't frightened. The thing that had caught my eye didn't inspire fear, only curiosity. I leaned in for a closer look and saw how tiny it was. It was helpless, sluggish, and struggling. I stopped and walked just to the edge of the concrete driveway. I got a better look at what I'd thought at first was a newborn kitten—but it wasn't. Surrounded by brush, trees, and straw in an open wooded area, the tiny creature was on the ground, struggling to crawl.

Moving even closer, I noticed it had a very long tail. My heart fluttered when the little thing stopped, its tiny head writhing as if it were in pain. Its tail had to be six inches long, the body appearing significantly smaller in comparison—maybe three inches. Its skin was light gray, almost white, and maybe hairless. I inched closer and realized it was a baby squirrel, but its fur was nothing like the brownish color of the ones I'd watched countless times swinging on branches and scampering on the ground.

> "Quietness is a treasure that is often undervalued, unexperienced, and underrated."

I thought to myself, "It's just a baby." It must have fallen out of its nest. The trees around it were tall and slender, and the branches were high and reached for the sky. I looked up, trying to see a nest, a mother squirrel, or some sign of where the squirrel had fallen. But there was no other movement. It was so very still and hushed all around me. There wasn't even the scurrying of other animals—just silence.

I watched. I thought of the loneliness of that moment. I imagined the overwhelming and painful fear this tiny newborn squirrel must have felt as it tottered on the edge of the nest before that unexpected, life-changing fall. I imagined the intense fortitude and inner drive that kept it crawling to survive after hitting the ground. I thought about us.

The baby squirrel started to move again. This time, its little back legs seemed to lose strength. My heart leaped, just as it does now as I think about what I witnessed. This was in 2020, and I still remember every detail. I still feel the emotions that resonated in me, as the sight made me think of God's Promise of Presence.

After just a few minutes, it was apparent that I was watching a struggle—an enormous and tragic struggle. The baby squirrel crawled a few inches again and then stopped. The bitter battle evident in each step captivated me.

I bore witness to this quiet and loud moment. It was a holy moment. Isolated and powerful. Unexpected and powerful. It dawned on me—rather, it dropped on me in that sacred moment—that I was the only one witnessing the last minutes of this life. And no one else was around for me to tell. Only later would I be able to tell anyone what I'd seen.

"I'm the only witness to this," I said, looking around helplessly. God then spoke loudly to me. It felt audible.

God said, "I see. I notice. I'm showing it to you, so you will know that I see you and every person in the world without a doubt. I see every person who feels alone and who is alone. I notice when people feel vulnerable, invisible, depressed, lost, and broken."

He said, "I notice. I see their birth because I know the exact time that each person will be born."

I was in complete awe; it was a feeling I'd never experienced before.

He continued, "I see the struggles. I see the heart. I see deep into the very crevices of every moment."

God said, "I see you. I feel you. I hear you. I saw this living thing, this baby squirrel, when it fell from the comfort and security of its nest. I saw it fall to the ground. I saw it struggling to the point of death."

The LORD's words from that day still resonate deeply with me. I can't help but weep as I write this.

His words were quiet but loud, and I completely understood what God decided to reveal to me. I continued watching the still-struggling baby squirrel. I knew it was preparing to die. I saw the last moments of that small, delicate creature. It curled into a fetal position. Looking like a baby, it died.

I felt an incredible stillness, and I was honored to have witnessed that moment alone with God.

Private Lessons, Private Battles

One day, Jesus tells His disciples, birds don't worry, and neither should you. Matthew 6:26 NIV gives us more details about this teaching; Jesus says, "Look at the birds. They don't plant, harvest, or store food in barns, for your heavenly Father feeds them. And aren't you far more valuable to him than they are? Can all your worries add a single moment to your life? And why worry about your clothing? Look at the lilies of the field and how they grow. They don't work or make their clothing, yet (King) Solomon, in all his glory, was not dressed as beautifully as they are. And if God cares so wonderfully for wildflowers that are here today and thrown into the fire tomorrow, he will certainly care for you."

I smile when I read the next thing Jesus says to His disciples, which shows that He notices you and what you need. He asks them, "Why do you have so little faith?"

I smile because I would have been in the crowd with them, needing to be taught and questioned to self-reflect on the level of my faith.

I might not have been like Nathanael, though maybe I would have been. In John 1:44–50 NIV, some of the brothers are talking about following Jesus. Here's how the conversation went:

Philip, like Andrew and Peter, was from the town of Bethsaida. Philip finds Nathanael and tells him, "We have found the one Moses wrote about in the Law, and about whom the prophets also wrote—Jesus of Nazareth, the son of Joseph."

"Nazareth! Can anything good come from there?" Nathanael asks.

"Come and see," says Philip.

When Jesus sees Nathanael approaching, He says of him, "Here truly is an Israelite in whom there is no deceit."

"How do you know me?" Nathanael asks.

Jesus answers, "I saw you while you were still under the fig tree before Philip called you."

Then Nathanael declares, "Rabbi, you are the Son of God; you are the king of Israel."

Incredible, isn't it? A boost of confidence! So we must live this life knowing that God sees and knows everything.

No one is a witness to every moment of our lives except God. Creator. Jehovah. Adonai. The Great and Magnificent God.

El Roi. It is not the "big bang theory" or "the universe" but He who is the Creator of all existence.

I learned so much that day, and so much was made clear to me. I am never alone, not even when I feel alone. I learned in the quietness of a random day. Quietness is a treasure that is often undervalued, unexperienced, and underrated. You and I don't need to worry about life.

God sees you.

God hears you.

God feels you.

In the next chapter, we'll talk about our place in the universe.

Reflection

But before we move on, let's reflect on and discuss what we've covered in this chapter:

1. After reading this chapter, what's your biggest takeaway?

2. In Genesis 2:18, Father God says it is not good for Adam (the only human being at the time) to be alone, and He did something about it. How does this make you feel?

3. Do you have instances in your life where you tried to hide from God's "view"? Explain.

4. What does the "Promise of Presence" mean to you?

5. Why do you think quietness is a treasure?

Honor what God is doing in you...

"For we are God's masterpiece. He has created us anew in Christ Jesus, so we can do the good things he planned for us long ago.
—Ephesians 2:10 NLT

"We were known and treasured by God right from the beginning. I know that I was not an afterthought, a mistake, or a mishap. I was not an unexpected accident born from a night of pleasure or a quick after-breakfast minute..."

CHAPTER TWO

Origins
From Where?

"We cannot escape our origins, however hard we try, those origins which contain the key—could we but find it—to all we later become."
—James Baldwin, American writer

You and I have a story. Separately defined, unique, but somehow divinely interwoven and intertwined. We have the power to choose and the ability to be inspired and motivated from within.

We live out our story, unable to tell it to anyone in its totality—only in snippets, frames, photos, and seasons. But we must be able to tell ourselves the facts and truths.

James Baldwin was a prolific writer and storyteller of some of the good, the bad, the ugly, and the messiness of life. This quote resonates with me deeply because Almighty God is the origin of everything known and unknown about life. Everything I write about in this book is based on this fact.

"In the beginning, God created the heavens and the earth. And the earth was without form and void, and darkness was upon the face of the deep. And the Spirit of God moved upon the face of the waters" Genesis 1–2 KJV. This is the origin that Moses (inspired by the Holy Spirit) wrote more than 3,000 years ago. And yes, I do realize that you may have an opposing view of how the world was created, but this is the context for what I have to tell you in this book.

FINDING ROOTS

We like to hear stories about where we came from. Commercial advertisements featuring personal stories and accounts of how someone met a relative or ancestor by searching on genealogy platforms are commonplace. The pride, passion, and love associated with discovering a family war hero, family pioneer, or long-lost relative match the commercial's soundtrack and imagery. Such commercials are filled with emotion and boast the immense value of knitting your origin story together to uncover family traits, successes, battles, and resilience. I must say, though, that these commercials do not tell the stories that involve enslavers, murderers, con men, or dysfunctional folks—none of the ugly. Quite frankly, many people would like to leave their unnamed war criminals, unspeakable acts, and unpopular relatives in the past, tearing that page out of history as if that would change history. It doesn't.

I remember when Alex Haley's 1976 book, *Roots: The Saga of an American Family*, was adapted into a television miniseries and aired on ABC in 1977. Haley's work of historical fiction depicted the generational origins of African American people from the African continent, who had been captured, enslaved, and sold worldwide. The television series chronicled how these people were brutalized, murdered, raped, extorted, manipulated, sold, and marginalized. I was in high school then, and my generation learned so much history about ourselves that had been hidden, undiscovered, and blotted out of the books we'd studied our whole lives in public schools. We learned about our ancestors' rituals of baby dedication while living under the imminent threat of being mercilessly separated and sold. We felt the pain and sheer will to survive, live, and hold on to family and culture. It was an excruciating experience to witness. But millions watched the series, and many more have viewed *Roots* since then. According to viewership data, 130 million viewers were glued to the television each week.

Roots provoked horror, anger, and empathy but, more importantly, inspired the search for origins and ancestry, which has changed the world. Haley will forever be known for his impact through *Roots* and other historical works.

Standing next to Mr. Haley and others who educated the masses is Henry Louis Gates. One of my favorite stations, PBS, started airing the documentary television series *Finding Your Roots* in 2012. Gates hosted this remarkable series, which combines expert researchers' work in genealogy and genetics to tell celebrity guests about their ancestry. If you've watched the show or read anything about it, you know that people discover many things about their family tree that they never knew. Sometimes, there are family members or facts Gates's guests may not be proud of. I have wondered if they wished Gates had revealed the outcomes privately instead of on public television.

We can feel this way about God too. Sometimes, He will make our private battle a public one that all can witness. Although it may be embarrassing in the moment, each of Gates's guests would ultimately adjust to the truth they'd discovered. Often, they admit they are better off knowing the entirety of their origins. One guest even said that the unexpected opened the door to understanding himself and his relationships.

Unfortunately, we cannot escape our origins. But sometimes, people think they can erase the truth by covering it up, rewriting it, or forbidding conversations about it.

SNAPSHOTS IN TIME

I often wonder about my own family origin. I have photos of my parents and grandmothers. I also have pictures of my grandfathers. When I look at their photographs side by side, I notice their distinctive demeanor and similar poses, as well as the well-tailored and dignified suits my grandfathers wore, all the while thinking that those were probably their Sunday best and not custom-tailored but off the rack of Montgomery Ward, JC Penney, or some local merchant that had in-house credit. Maybe they'd spent a month's wages on those suits.

I have read of the oppression of the 1900s and wonder what it was like for my grandparents and, later, my parents as young children. Separate but equal was constitutional, and other attempts to keep Black people from living freely in this country were the practice of the day. But these tactics could not break or destroy their hope or desire to prove their place in this world.

Origins: From Where?

Looking at the faces of my grandfathers, I wonder: What did they find joy in? What were their private battles, and do we fight the same ones? I wonder about my paternal grandfather, whom I never met. What was he really like?

My paternal grandfather was born in 1909. I never met him, and he died in Brooklyn in 1998.

I don't wonder nearly as much about my maternal grandfather, who was born in 1900, because, like my grandmothers, I saw him almost every day when I was a child. After our parents divorced, he was at our home a lot. He would almost always come to our house with groceries or something else to help my mom raise the seven of us. He took care of us, and I think I became a coffee lover because of him.

He had a ritual of sorts when making his coffee—morning, afternoon, or evening. I would watch intently from underneath the kitchen chair most of the time; that alone tells you how young I was. Granddaddy Herring, we called him, as his name was George Washington Herring. He was a pastor, and many people referred to him as Reverend Herring. He would be dressed in black slacks, a crisp white shirt, black suspenders, black socks, and shiny black Stacey Adams—and granddaddy always wore a fedora hat. His socks had something that looked like the garters the women at that time wore to keep their stockings in place. He was meticulous and intentional in all he did. Now that I think about it, he liked order, structure, and proper use and function. He was well dressed at all times and always had a white handkerchief. He was what I would consider a gentleman of his time. He smoked a pipe and wore eyeglasses, and his all-gray hair was a portrait. Completing the image was a pocket watch.

Granddaddy Herring would set the kitchen table with a cup, saucer, small plate, knife, fork, and spoon. Taking the butter dish out of the refrigerator and placing it on the table were also part of his morning ritual. He'd then place the coffee pot on the stove to boil. While he waited for the kettle's soft whistle that signaled it was ready, he would take out his pipe, fill it with tobacco, and light it. After a few long puffs, the room would fill with the familiar aroma that I liked. After a few minutes of smoking, he'd make a slice of toast. He would always scrape the piece of toast with a butter knife, place it on his plate, and then spread butter on it. Right at that time, the coffee pot would start whizzing, filling our small kitchen with yet another lovely aroma, prompting my grandfather to rise. From my vantage point beneath the kitchen chair, his movements always seemed to be brimming with dignity and intent. I was rarely alone in watching him; my sister and two younger brothers would also be in the room. But I think I was the only one captivated by my grandfather's coffee ritual.

I would watch him take the hot coffee pot from the stove and place it on the table before him. And I'm telling you, when sitting down, he'd pause and look at his table setting, as if admiring the beauty of the simple things in life, before picking up the coffee pot to pour his first cup. I'd watch so intently, mesmerized by the steaming hot concoction in his favorite coffee cup. Granddaddy Herring would add some cane sugar and then pour from a can of Carnation creamer till the brew matched his light caramel complexion. At least, that's the connection I made. It makes me laugh even now to think of my six-year-old self's correlations.

I swear my grandfather stirred his coffee exactly ten times before he was satisfied. I'm not kidding. The whole thing seemed so serious to me as a kid. After mixing, he would pour just a little bit of coffee into the saucer and then drink from it. The grand tasting, I used to think. The perfect cup.

I'd imagine the taste; that alone was intriguing. Each time, we would ask, "Granddaddy, can we have some coffee?"

"No, coffee makes you black," he would say, laughing as if he'd heard a good joke for the first time. I wouldn't know there's a book with the same name, *Coffee Makes You Black*, until I was older. Granddaddy was light-skinned; his father was of German descent, and his mother was a Native American. We were much darker than he was, but that didn't stop us from asking him for a teaspoon of coffee. We didn't care. We kept asking, and every now and then he would give each of us a teaspoon.

One of the reasons I enjoy coffee is the joy it gave my grandfather. A simple pleasure in tumultuous times. A simple pleasure in times when hard decisions had to be made. A simple pleasure in times when sacrifice was routine for survival.

I come from people who lived at or below the poverty line. This was not uncommon given the socio-economic makeup of America, the history of slavery, racial politics and injustice, voter suppression, the Ku Klux Klan, segregation, Jim Crow, the civil rights movement, recessions, depressions, natural disasters, separations, divorces, tragedy—the list goes on. I come from people who are resilient, optimistic, and passionate. And most importantly, I come from people who believed in moral standards but even more profoundly believed in God and His Son, Jesus Christ.

There are seven and a half billion people in the world, and millions are curious about their origins—their ancestry and heritage. I am one of them. I traced my family tree on my father's side, hoping to learn about the grandfather I had never met or known anything about. His name was Roy Terry, and he was married to my grandmother. They had three children together, and my father was the oldest. I wanted to learn more about my father's lineage because legend had it that, when my dad was a child, my grandfather had to leave the town one night after a dangerous situation, never to return. He fled to New York, changed his identity, and started a new life with a new family.

I've learned that people make decisions and choices that permanently affect other people and their bloodlines. People make mistakes, have regrets, and often try to self-correct to live, survive, and thrive. It happened in my family, myself included, and I would guess it did in yours too.

Every person is battling something at any given moment in life. It's not merely the difficult moments in life but how you handle the difficult moments in life. My grandfather probably thought of his Florida family every day of his life, tucked it away in his heart, and lived with those emotions until the day he died. I don't know

Origins: From Where?

the specifics of why he had to flee Florida, but he left his wife and young children because he saw no other way. I can only imagine his pain from that decision, which must have lasted until his last breath. My grandmother Daisy's pain, my own father's pain, his siblings' pain—that

> "Our origins contain the key to all we later become. I found the key."

of everyone in our bloodline. Everyone has to battle something, but God knows how to help us.

More than sixty years after Grandfather Roy fled, my father and his siblings were called. His New York family notified my Florida family of his passing and they went. This was a really compassionate act, and it means that Grandfather Roy must of have spoken of his Florida family to his New York family.

Private battles. Private lessons. Everyone has them. I was always curious about my paternal grandfather. This saga made me even more curious, and I wanted to know more, especially years later when my own father died.

However, I didn't find much and just sat with the knowledge of what I do know about my family. I have blood ties to many people I don't know, but I have relationships with those I do know. Though DNA says my origins can be traced back to Nigeria, Togo, and even the United Kingdom, I am okay with the many unknowns and knowns.

Sometimes, not knowing our family ancestry leaves a void that we believe is unfillable. Even trauma experienced at the hands of a family member, which you may think cannot be healed, leaves behind an emptiness. But the truth is that, no matter what, Father God can heal and fill even the unexplainable void you feel inside. After all, we began with Him. *He is the key to our origin.*

In a world so obsessed with seeking answers but that often does not find any, the one question that can be asked and actually answered is this: Where do I come from? Though many don't believe it, the answer is that you came from God; it is still an eternal truth. When you embrace this truth, your life can transcend situational troubles, cyclical decisions, maladjustments, and grief. You will live on a higher level as a spiritually mature person with a deep consciousness of God.

We were known and treasured by God right from the beginning. I know that I was not an afterthought, a mistake, or a mishap. I was not an unexpected accident born from a night of pleasure or a quick after-breakfast minute. Rather, I came from the eternal chambers of God.

THE FAITH OF MY FATHERS

When I think of my origins, of where I actually began, I wonder who my ancestors were as people.. Though I don't know the answers to those questions, I am so thankful that they passed on the teachings of their faith to me. I have so many stories about my grandmothers, aunts, uncles, siblings, and cousins, all of whom have left an imprint on my life. Not to mention the indelible impression left by my parents. But what is most important for me is what they have passed on about my spiritual origin—I came from God.

They talked about God, creation, and Jesus Christ. Along with others who lived where I grew up, they spoke of loving and serving God. They didn't, nor could they, force God on me. They did talk about and try to walk the path of their faith. Never did they pretend to be perfect. I've heard people say they don't want to force God on their children as the children can find God independently. But they expose their children to harmful lifestyles and attitudes and expect them to be perfect. Many decide not to tell their children about a faith that will last throughout their lives. But God is gracious and kind, and when we sincerely search for Him we will find Him.

I am so grateful that I was taught about Jesus Christ at a young age. I made the decision to follow Jesus Christ, just like every person who hears the gospel will need to decide. To be clear, I have not been perfect. I've made an incredible amount of mistakes and sinned in my life since deciding to follow Jesus.

I had heard a lot about my spiritual origins, but it wasn't until I accepted Jesus Christ honestly for myself that I knew He is real. What I mean is that I knew and believed in the history of creation as recorded in the Book of Genesis, but I never saw myself clearly in the grand scheme of things until I studied more deeply and decided I wanted to know God.

Baldwin said we cannot escape our origins, however hard we try. Our origins contain the key to all we later become. I found the key. I now understand that my spiritual origin informs and weighs heavily on how I think, how I act, how I live, how I love, and how I fit into the world. It affects my private life and public life. Everything about me is governed by it. I learned that it happens on the inside before it shows up on the outside. I want my life perspective to be rooted in the truth of God's Word (my spiritual origin), not solely in my natural origin.

ORIGINS: FROM WHERE?

Reflection

Before we move on to the next chapter, let's reflect on and discuss what we've covered in this chapter:

1. After reading this chapter, do you struggle to trust in the Bible as God's words for your origin story? Why or why not?

2. Read Psalm 139:1–18. What resonates with you?

3. People may describe you in many ways, but it is more important to believe what God has said about you. Write a word in each box that describes you:

"We often want external answers to internal questions. We want someone to help us understand what only the Holy Spirit can work out in us, for us, and through us. Deep down, you may want someone to tell you what they see..."

CHAPTER THREE

Private Practice
No Degree Required

"But when you pray, go away by yourself, shut the door behind you, and pray to your Father in private. Then your Father, who sees everything, will reward you."
—Matthew 6:6 NLT

What you practice in private will show up in public. You've probably heard the phrase, "Character is who you are when nobody can see you or when no one is looking." Character is developed when no one is looking, when no one can see you, and truthfully, it is produced privately. The beginning of a quest for our higher selves begins in private. The spiritual connection our hearts and souls seek begins in private. The search for forgiveness and peace with God starts in private. The search for purpose and meaning in life begins in private. Our interaction with and connection to God is a private practice. Experiencing Jesus is a private practice.

Matthew 6:6 is striking, it reads: "But when you pray, go away by yourself, shut the door behind you, and pray to your Father in private. Then your Father, who sees everything, will reward you." Let's take a look at the same verse in the Message translation:

Private Lessons, Private Battles

"Here's what I want you to do: Find a quiet, secluded place so you won't be tempted to role-play before God. Just be there as simply and honestly as you can manage. The focus will shift from you to God, and you will begin to sense his grace."

Matthew 6:6 leads us to a powerful place of understanding, if and when we practice what it says. Behind closed doors in the privacy of our own hearts in faith is where we learn the keys to living and discover the truth of God's promises.

We often want external answers to internal questions. Sometimes we want someone to help us understand what only the Holy Spirit can work out in us, for us, and through us.

Deep down, you may want someone to tell you what they see. You want confirmation of what you already know. You may wonder if anyone "sees" the real you. Privately, you've questioned faith. Privately, you may have deep doubts. Privately, you may feel rejected, angry, and abandoned. Privately, you're struggling with something. Privately, you wonder if God sees you or even hears you. And privately, you may have contradictions, inconsistencies, pain, worry, turmoil, torment, conflicts, arrogance, and even bitterness. These are tough conversations to have, but inward insecurities may be the culprit always trying to disrupt your peace and rob you of your dreams. Maybe you even find yourself saying "yes" when your mind screams "no." Privately, we have questions whose answers are unknown but desperately needed. Many of us have not sat down long enough in a resting place to listen and learn what only the Holy Spirit can give us.

Do you ever just sit with yourself to explore the nudges and prompts you're feeling inside? That quiet but loud voice that says, "Leave, stop talking, pray now, humble yourself, try again, take the class, do something different, build up your faith, go for that job, start that business, take a vacation, get some rest, change the way you think, accept the help offered, end that relationship, take a different route"—the list can go on for pages.

But, in truth, you're the only one who can recognize the whispers, messages, warnings, and lessons stirring inside you. The lessons push up inside you like a seedling pushing through the soil weeks, if not years, after being buried.

Yes, you are functioning. You're grinding. You're performing outward actions and expectations, but something is not right, and you know it.

There is an internal conflict that you've not yet been able to put your finger on because you haven't given it any real attention. You sense the instability, but you keep doing what you're doing—like everyone else, you assume. We keep doing what we're doing, what everyone else seems to be doing, often delaying or missing the very things we need on the inside.

LIVING MY BEST LIFE?

You are achieving your goals. You have the car you want; you have a plan for your dream house; you have a good job; you're vegan now; you have friends; you've had a bomb birthday photoshoot; and you slay every time you step out. Classes are going great—As

Private Lessons, Private Battles

and Bs this semester. Your Amazon boxes are coming in on time. You finished the vision board. Your children are doing well. You've finally established a workout routine. You drink a healthy smoothie every day, and you've stopped having fast food for dinner. Not to mention you are starting to pray more. And, of course, you have the correct number of followers on social media, and you are definitely feeling good about yourself. But…not really. Something is speaking to you.

"Living my best life" is a popular hashtag for every vacation, staycation, and staged and filtered photo. I have a T-shirt with the same message, and that is when I started to question this thing. Am I living my best life?

Perhaps the quote should be "Living my best life on the outside." Life is a journey, absolutely—an inward journey. My grandmama used to say, "All that glitters ain't gold," and you know it's true as well as I do. So let's face it and address the elephant in everybody's room; as the great poet Langston Hughes penned in "Mother to Son," "Life for me ain't been no crystal stair."

As much as we love filtered pictures of outward perfection, that's not the truth, is it?

I think of the scripture that says the LORD seeks truth in the inward parts, and that is where the actual work has to occur to let me live my best life. I battled with this for many years before recognizing the lesson God was teaching me.

Living my best life is not singularly determined by my professional achievements, my financial portfolio, wardrobe, passport stamps, or any other symbol of material achievement. Rather, it is determined solely by how I live in every moment and how I navigate the worst and the best times of my life.

Are you living your best life?

Do you have an internal conflict that you're pushing down and covering up to avoid the private confrontation you must have with yourself? We push it off and delay it now, but it will inevitably happen.

Maybe today is the day. Right now. Right this minute.

Ezra Taft Benson said, "Some of the greatest battles will be fought within the silent chambers of your own soul."

Experiencing and dealing with personal battles are undeniable parts of being human. Being conflicted, confronted, and confused at times are all part of human nature. We have probably been in a billion battles from birth until now, privately and personally. Life is a series of personal and private struggles that no one else knows about until it spills over into the atmosphere. When we lash out, act out, breakdown, or say things we cannot retract. These may be the fiercest and the most painful; and, I would say some of the most profound and severe in our inner lives—the inner corners, canals, shadows, and quiet areas of our very being. The places that only the Holy Spirit can enter and deal with.

Our closest loved ones often cannot detect the shaking and unearthing that is going on right next to them. Though they are physically close, other people cannot always see and discern the private battles of another person. Or, to put it better, they cannot experience the personal struggles of another person. They can empathize, of course, but some fights are ours and ours alone.

Close your eyes. Just close them. Tell me. Who is inside of you other than you? No one. The reality of "being" is apparent. The truth of individuality is clear. And the place of privacy is also clear. As I stated in the previous chapter, our lives didn't begin the day we were conceived or the day we were born. We originated in the mind of God. We are His creation.

Close your eyes. Have you welcomed the Creator into the space where He already exists? Have you accepted and acknowledged Him as the source and your source for living your best life?

OPEN UP

How do you nurture a relationship with God? You cannot see Him, but you grapple to feel Him, if nothing else. How do you?

I discovered a battle in myself about these very questions, and I had to learn their answers. I learned a lot in church, but I learned even more in my private practice.

How do I have a relationship with God anyway? The only relationship I could understand earlier in my life were those with people. And honestly, they weren't that good, so I struggled with relationships. It was hard for me to connect with people on a personal level. It just was. In all honesty, I had to learn about relationships beyond the temporary level. But I learned to value them. I also learned how to become closer to God in an authentic way—in a relationship. In church, I heard what I interpreted as a "formula" for a relationship with God. I do not blame anyone for how I interpreted it. No blame. I learned and developed a more mature faith. I was often expecting from people things that only the Holy Spirit can do.

Looking back, I realize I grew up hearing about the "formula" to reach God for most of my life. "Do it this way, or else" is how I interpreted what I heard. This used to be my private practice formula:

Practice 1. Get up at zero dark thirty to seek His face (in the military, zero dark thirty was very, very early in the morning).

Practice 2. Wash my face and prepare myself as if I were meeting an earthly king.

Practice 3. Always lie on the floor before the LORD.

Practice 4. Pray loudly, using the words and style you hear at church (if you are not loud and aggressive, you are not passionate, and you don't mean the words coming out of your mouth).

In a way, the truth was found in what I'd heard, as I have listed. I realize that how I "heard" it might be how many people—not everyone—my age at the time "heard" it. So I believe it is vital for us to learn how to have meaningful relationships and, more importantly, a real relationship with God. My intentions were sincere, albeit religious, my faith was real, and God helped me. I'm not saying anything was wrong with what I came up with as I learned through this pattern and practiced how to become closer to God.

NO FORMULAS

> "The rabbi was waiting patiently. I looked at him and said with confidence and inner strength, "I need to forgive myself."

According to Farlex's Free Dictionary, a formula is "a set form of words, as for stating something authoritatively, for indicating procedure to be followed, or for prescribed use on some ceremonial occasion." The next part got my attention even more:

"Any fixed or conventional method or approach." Boom. I was shaken. It was life to me.

Trying to follow a spiritual "formula" was a misstep. Don't get me wrong, I didn't have a script or pretense, but it did feel awkward and burdensome to try to follow such a strict set of guidelines. I struggled, and I was frustrated. But God worked in me, through me, and for me because I was sincere.

What you need is not a "formula" but a sincere desire to know God. For El Roi says, "If you seek me with all of your heart, you will find me." What I learned early on in life then translated into a deeper meaning:

<u>Getting up early (zero dark thirty)</u> doesn't restrict me to a specific time; it means starting my day by seeking Him.

<u>Washing my face</u> means to begin focusing with a refreshed and respectful approach to enter the Holy and Sovereign Presence of the Only True and Living God.

<u>Laying before the LORD</u> on the floor doesn't mean I'm restricted to this particular posture. My inner resolve should be that I need Him entirely and above everyone and everything else. It means complete obeisance to God—that is, respect, submission, and reverence, not just in physical posture but inwardly as well. So let's lay before the Lord in complete submission to Him as a matter of practice and understanding.

<u>Praying with fervor</u> means praying passionately and sincerely from the heart; sometimes, it may get loud, and sometimes, it may remain silent. Consider Hannah praying in 1 Samuel 1: her mouth was moving, tears streaming down her face, as she poured her heart out to God, but there was no audible sound. Prayer requires no title and no appointment. I relish this privilege and honor that is given to us independent of time, location or physicality. You could be leading a corporate prayer or praying in your closet; it is a private matter that is effective only when it comes from a pure place.

We have unlimited access to the Sovereign God who moves the world—every day, everywhere, and at any time. 1 Thessalonians 5:17 NLT says to never stop praying, even when you don't feel like it. Prayer is a weapon and a point of access that we cannot afford to downplay or disregard. I know some people are saying, "I'm tired of praying." The devil likes this and wants this way of thinking to catch on even more and spread like a wildfire knowing that if you keep saying it where others can hear it, more and more people will throw down one of the most potent weapons in life's journey. The other is faith. Faith and prayer are a couple. They must co-exist.

We are approaching the highest authority in prayer. Keep praying. Silence the noise, and bow down and pray from a pure place. God is Sovereign, and we are not. He is fully able and powerful to handle every detail and every matter. God has all the information about everything and everybody; we do not. Pray.

PRIVATE DEVOTION

One of the things I grew up doing that I did not categorize as part of a "formula" is reading, studying, and meditating on God's word. This practice has always been an absolute essential for life. Though I have not been perfect, God's Word has always been powerful and prevailing in my life. God's Word has carried me and sustained me. I learned that religious talk cannot overcome issues, but faith talk will. Speaking God's Word in faith changes you from the inside out. It is why I have a relationship with God—through it all.

What about you? Do you have a relationship with God that you have built over the course of your life? Is it only religious and learned?

Jesus says to the expert in the law who asked him which is the greatest commandment, "Love the Lord your God with all your heart and with all your soul and with all your mind. This is the first and greatest commandment" Matthew 22:35–38 NIV.

All means all or nothing—nothing excluded and everything included in every situation. Life can get so overwhelming and crowded. Too much information, too many voices. Have you ever felt as if life is pressurized and just too much? Honestly, I did. And I needed to slow my life down and improve my quality of life. To do that, I had to understand a fundamental truth that we talk about a lot: Devotion. I asked myself, "Am I devoted to God, really?"

In that season of my life, I spent many years crying, loathing, and dreading. I looked prosperous, and I functioned well. I achieved a few things, and I own a few things, but the quality of a person's life is determined, in my view, by what's happening inside, not outside.

Things can appear one way externally while being something else entirely inside.

I prayed to God about my internal matters because, while I had things and opportunities aplenty, something was not quite right inside.

A DIFFERENT LOCATION

It was 2018, our first time in London and it was everything I'd imagined and so much more. We were invited by our friends, who are practically family, and we had a blast. After ten days in London, we headed to the airport to visit family in Germany for a few weeks. As we entered the departure concourse, I saw a quote spread across the entire wall of the waiting area: "Travel is not getting away from your life but getting to your life. It is not the length of life but the depth." I felt the quiet loudness of God speaking to me in that moment. He hears us talking to Him. He already knows what we're going to say before we say it—before we ask it. He answered my questions. That day was a turning point. I became more aware of God and knew He was the answer.

I noticed that my private battles, the questioning-contending-conflicting-troubling-struggling inner turmoil, would bring me peace and reveal a private lesson or insight that would draw me closer to God. And then I realized that sometimes, I couldn't identify the personal battle that was raging inside me. It was just happening. That changed when we traveled to Israel a few years ago. We were so excited. We travel abroad frequently, but something about the thought of walking through the Bible invigorated me.

Believe it or not, I broke my foot the night before our flight! My husband thought we should go to the emergency room, but I couldn't imagine sitting there all night before taking a long flight. Despite the pain, I told myself I did not break it. I have a high pain threshold and experienced mid-level pain for most of the trip. Still,

I don't regret not going to the emergency room. I'd invested a few years back in some good running shoes, so I laced them up snug enough to support my foot in expectation of a lot of walking.

(Don't be like me! Go to the emergency room!)

Israel was a twelve-day trip, and I had no idea what God had in store for me 6,382 miles away from home.

I was unaware of the impending confrontation. I couldn't have predicted what would happen a few days into the trip, at the Jordan River.

2 Kings 5 gives you a glimpse into the geography and ecosystem of the Jordan River during the time the high-ranking military officer Naaman was there *not for baptism but for healing*. Have you read about Naaman's dislike of and indignant attitude about dipping himself in the muddy Jordan River instead of being met and touched by the prophet? I understand. It would have been easier and cleaner to skip the Jordan. The river was muddy; there were flies everywhere.

Hundreds of people in different groups from different regions had come there to experience the baptism in the same murky waters Jesus had.

I stood in the Jordan River, excited about being baptized in the same river as my LORD and Savior! I was brimming with excitement, jubilance, and, honestly, all the religious fervor expected on such an occasion. When we first arrived at the site, the rabbi explained to our group an aspect of baptism that I'd never heard before. He said we could choose to immerse ourselves in the water or have him dip us into the water. Whichever choice we made, we could share it with him when it was our turn.

My husband was assisting the rabbi, helping people into the water and standing by as needed. We sang hymns while the others stepped into the water where the rabbi was standing. Around an hour later, everyone else in our group—about twelve people—was baptized, and it was our turn. Team Jones.

I could not have imagined or expected what happened next. Even now, when writing this down, I had to pause to take a deep breath.

We walked out into the water, where the rabbi was standing. I was speaking in tongues (using my heavenly language!) and getting ready to be baptized when the rabbi said to me, "Stop!"

"Wait. What?" I thought.

What could interrupt such a "sacred and biblical moment" in the Jordan River? After all, he was a rabbi—and we were not in a church revival. What could be happening? I was on one wavelength, and the rabbi was on another. I was literally in my world, and God was interrupting my plans.

The rabbi said again, "Stop! Just stop. We can't move on. You can't move forward." He was speaking to just me and not us—Team Jones!

Again, I thought, "Wait, what? Oh God!"

I was mortified. I honestly had no idea what was happening. I looked at Nathan with a pleading expression—that look you give your love, and he knows to come to the rescue?
Yes? No, not this time.

Nathan's face said, "Why are you looking at me? Don't look at me; he ain't talking to me. This is between you and the LORD; I ain't in it. It's your business."

"I'm on my own out here," I thought. I settled myself and shot the rabbi a questioning look. The private battle had become a public battle, but I didn't know that yet. I couldn't even identify the struggle that had been going on—only that, even though I'd been praying about it for a long time, something was not okay within me. I couldn't put words to it; I couldn't share what I didn't understand.

The rabbi insisted on pausing the baptism, claiming, "God is telling me you have the spirit of grief, and you cannot move on."

Yes, that is what he told me.

I was shocked.

I was ashamed and embarrassed.

I almost didn't include this incident in this book, but I have to share the whole story.

Honestly, I felt some real religious embarrassment when the rabbi said this in front of my husband. No one else could hear the alarms blaring inside me. I looked around me, wondering if anyone else had heard what the rabbi had said. Fight or flight? No, more like run and hide!

"I now realize why you were the last for me to minister to," the rabbi said, ostensibly to us both but looking at me.

I felt ambushed, my mind growing frenzied. "I didn't sign up for this," I thought. "Not here, not now." I repented privately to the LORD for feeling how I was feeling. I repented for the arrogance and self-righteousness I harbored inside myself.

Listen, a lot was going on inside me. I'd gone there to get baptized, and instead, I'd been put on the spot.

I said to the LORD, "What is this? Are you really doing this here, right now?"

I honestly didn't know what the LORD was doing, but I did know it was a holy moment like no other—in public!

So I prayed inside to honor the moment and accept the LORD's work in me.

The rabbi continued. "Do you need to forgive anyone? Is there something that you haven't faced?"

I didn't find it difficult to forgive people, so that didn't seem to be the issue.

I tried thinking about a solution to this quandary, but only escape was on the forefront of my mind.

I would have literally walked on water just to get out of there. I looked around, across the water, and about twenty feet away, the country of Jordan sprawled out before me.

We had entered the water from the Israeli side and now faced another country. Crowds of people were on both sides. I thought they'd all heard the rabbi interrogating me. I was puzzled, thinking, "Why am I being cross-examined about something I wasn't even aware of in the middle of the Jordan River?"

The rabbi was waiting for me to answer with a pleading expression. He seemed to want to help me, but he could only wait. Again, I felt trapped and pressured to answer. The rabbi was not budging.

I prayed silently, "Right now, LORD? Right here? What are you asking me?"

Left with no choice, I decided to face the moment. I humbled myself; I had to. I murmured, "Okay, LORD," accepting what was happening. I then began to really think about it. God had brought me to that moment to *help me help myself.*

"Yes, Lord," I thought.

I was determined to search my heart and mind for the answer. It was a moment of spiritual and personal clarity. I thought of different people who'd wronged me, but I had forgiven them. I didn't harbor any grudges. I was determined to answer the LORD and face whatever He was teaching me. I thought more—and it hit me like the proverbial ton of bricks: I had not forgiven myself. I'd always thought forgiveness was to be doled out to other people. Matthew 6:15 NIV reads, "But if you do not forgive others their sins, your Father in heaven will not forgive your sins."

It had never occurred to me to give myself grace, care, and forgiveness. I'd packed away my regret and grief for sins, mistakes, bad decisions, and moral failures. I'd never discussed my pain with anyone, not even God, though I did ask Him for forgiveness. He forgave me, but I was still carrying it around privately.

I'd been in mourning for many years without ever realizing it. I was nurturing my grief and regret privately. What does that mean? Nurturing means caring for and encouraging the development of someone or something; similarly, nurturing hope, love, regret, or grief means caring for and encouraging the development of these emotions. On the outside, I was going about my business, but on the inside, I was stuck and struggling to move forward. Looking back, I ask you: "What are you putting forth publicly but nurturing privately?"

Before that day in the Jordan River, I couldn't identify what it was. That private battle I couldn't name? It was unforgiveness. I functioned outwardly, but I had been crippled in many ways by guilt and regret, which showed up as grief. Perhaps no one else could see it, but I did—and God did. I couldn't explain it, but God knew and He had a plan to pull me out of it.

I think of Paul the Apostle. Perhaps he was dealing with self-forgiveness too, but he was moving forward. 1 Corinthians 15:9–10 NIV tells us his words: "For I am the least of the apostles and do not even deserve to be called an apostle, because I persecuted the church of God. But by the grace of God, I am what I am…"

The rabbi was waiting patiently. I looked at him and said with confidence and inner strength, "I need to forgive myself."

"Okay, we can move forward now," he responded.

There was no hugging or crying or any emotional display—simply sincere words, just like that.

What he'd said to everyone earlier in the day resonated with me in that moment: "You can choose to immerse yourself or have me immerse you." Submission and surrender came to my mind. I was relieved.

We were baptized, and the experience was beyond anything I could have imagined.

As we walked out of the water, I was free from what I hadn't known had held me in bondage for so many years.

I learned that we could be off track and out of alignment with God in our religious mindsets and habits, regardless of good intentions. Imagine picture frames of various sizes. We often frame God in the lens and scope of our experiences, education, denomination, perceptions, culture, prejudices, political affiliations, religious upbringing, and intellect so that we can understand and be comfortable with Him. We, in effect, attempt to place limits on God, who created everything. In attempting to put God in a box, we are putting ourselves in a box. I've learned we can be religiously consistent and wrong at the same time. We are imperfect, but He is perfect and kind to us.

IN SYNC

What if you don't have a relationship with God right now? You can have a relationship with God through faith in Jesus Christ. He already knows your name. Don't you want Him to know you? Don't you want to know Him? You have full access to God. The scripture tells us that when Christ died on the cross, the temple's veil was torn and ripped. Jesus tore down the wall of partition, and we don't need to confess to a priest to have a relationship with God in Jesus Christ. Start your private practice; no degree or formula is required. Start by accepting that you can meet Jesus Christ anywhere at any time. You can be open and honest with Him. You can come boldly before Him, have an honest conversation and pour out your heart.

Believe in Jesus Christ and that He is the only son of God. He came to die for our sins on the cross. Knowing that everyone would not accept Him, He died anyway. Knowing that He wants to reconcile with every soul but that everyone does not want His will, He died anyway. You have this opportunity to confess your sins and be forgiven. This is beautiful. This is the start of an evolving and transformational relationship. God is still calling your name. He has called your name from the beginning. It's not complicated.

A relationship with God is like no other. For thousands of years, human beings have complicated things that are in truth uncomplicated. I chuckle when I hear "it's complicated" repeatedly in television shows or even random conversations. It seems that this phrase has taken on a life of its own. Unfortunately, people keep saying "it's complicated", and perhaps it becomes what they say. Well, having a relationship with God is not complicated.

You choose this most divine and life-giving relationship through faith.

What God teaches you privately will show up in your life.

Reflection

Before we move on to the next chapter, let's reflect on and discuss what we've covered in this chapter:

1. What is one of your main takeaways from this chapter?

2. Do you feel awkward coming before the LORD alone, like outside of a church service? What can you do to ease this feeling?

3. How do you rate the quality of your life, and where have you placed value? Be honest.

4. What about forgiveness? Is there an issue causing you to feel grief? Be honest.

5. After reading this chapter, do you recognize a private practice you should add to draw you closer to God?

6. Prayer is our highest honor, our highest privilege and power. We have complete and unimpeded access to the God of Heaven– the Sovereign LORD. How does this make you feel?

"There is power in noticing. Not just for navigating to the next location but for navigating life to gain and sustain peace, joy, and solace. We are training ourselves not to notice and to be in a mode of constant distraction, to the detriment of our whole being."

CHAPTER FOUR

The Power of Noticing
Did You See That?

"Sometimes you must change your seat, your mind, your perspective to see differently and notice what you didn't see before. When you do, you will increase your power."
—Daisy Jones

There was a long line to get into the seminar and I was excited to hear the speaker. The place was crowded and I couldn't see around the man sitting in front of me. I shifted around in my seat, and my view opened up dramatically. I could see the stage and the speaker, which somehow seemed to improve my hearing.

WHAT DID YOU MISS?

We drove by the restaurant three times before noticing it was at the corner—big as day. The problem was that our destination blended in a little too well with the other stores and cafes around it. The traffic was congested, and we were moving too fast to notice. Although we had directions and were looking for this particular restaurant, we just kept driving by it. Something wasn't right. Or was it? Maybe we'd gone around in a circle three times because we had something else on our minds, making us blind to our true surroundings. In any case, we didn't notice the bright red sign for the restaurant right there on the curb until the fourth go-around. Indeed, two people looking for the same thing should have seen that we'd passed it three times.

We all tend not to notice things or even people, especially in our culture of rushing to rush.

Marketers are counting on us not noticing the subtle changes in the size of products. Have you seen how the bottle, the bag, and the box have become smaller while the price has increased? Have you noticed the ingredients in the food you buy, and how the font size is smaller, but the list is longer? Have you noticed a change in the quality of food items?

Have you noticed that most people stare at a smartphone or device during dinner instead of talking? Adults and children ride in vehicles with their heads down on phones and tablets most of the time, paying no attention to their surroundings or the scenery. There is power in noticing—Not just for navigating to the next location but for navigating life to gain and sustain peace, joy, and solace. We are training ourselves not to notice and to be in a mode of constant distraction, to the detriment of our whole being.

WHAT DO YOU HEAR? LISTEN

Divine notifications. My phone just made the sound I chose last week from my sounds and notifications. It's unique, and I selected it to distinguish between email and voicemail notifications. That made me think about divine notifications—a feeling that heaven is speaking. I've noticed this feeling of course when praying, studying God's Word, and in a worship service setting; but also when I've seen something, while talking to people, watching television or a movie, listening to a lecture, reading, just out walking, and at other seemingly random times. It's a pause for a wisdom nugget, a warning, an idea, a strategy, enlightenment, and a variety of life-giving insights. We all get them.

Do you get divine notifications? How do you respond?

What are you noticing? Are you able to notice God's nudging and urging?

Most of us have been graced with five senses to experience life in remarkable ways. Why do we miss so much that has been given to enrich our lives from the inside out? We rush, are too busy, and have too many obligations and distractions. This was true for me as well, until I recognized what I was missing. Now, each day, I am conscious of maintaining boundaries to make sure I won't return to that state. I realize we sometimes have to change our seat to see differently. You'll have to change your position (view and/or mindset) or shift your body (life) to see around someone or something. When you move, not only do you see more, see differently, and increase your focus, but you will also notice something you did not see before.

Can I tell you something? In addition to our five natural senses, we have the Holy Spirit, who will teach us and allow us to see, notice, hear, perceive, and understand in ways beyond our natural abilities. In John 14:16–17 MSG, Jesus says, "I will talk to the Father, and he'll provide you another Friend so that you will always have someone with you. This Friend is the Spirit of Truth. The godless world can't take Him in because it doesn't have eyes to see Him and doesn't know what to look for. But you know Him already because He has been staying with you and will even be in you!"

I want to tell you something that will change your life from this moment on:

- God created you; therefore, you possess the power to notice and hear when God speaks to you.

- You can discover, through the help of the Holy Spirit, your friend, lessons that can only be taught by Him. Not only lessons but abilities that are only empowered by Him. He is essential.

- You will notice the Hand of God and the Presence of God.

- Through the help of the Holy Spirit, you will develop insights that will nourish your soul and mind.

- You are a whole being, made in the image and likeness of Father God. There's no need to compartmentalize or box up any part of who you are.

- You have a unique assignment on this earth that only you can complete. It is not because of your actions, appearance, accomplishments, triumphs, or failures, but a result of the divine purposes that God placed in you long before you were born.

PAYING ATTENTION

Watching birds and squirrels is a powerful reminder that nothing in our lives is too small or insignificant for the LORD to notice. God wants a deep and loving relationship with you. As I said earlier, He initiated this relationship and wants you to be keenly aware of His desire to interact, communicate, and care for you in every moment and every situation of your life. God wants you to know He is present. He wants you to know there is nothing that can separate you from His love. He wants you to know you have His attention—even when you're wrong.

> "Why do we miss so much that has been given to enrich our lives from the inside out?"

God doesn't condone sin. He hates it, but there is no mess you're in that can prevent Him from speaking to you or saving you. He knows what type of mess has captivated and paralyzed you. He knows the kind of messes we struggle with, and He wants to pull us out.

God knows every little thing about you. He notices every detail. He pays more attention to you than you do. Believe it. Do you know the exact number of strands of hair on your head? He does. Jesus describes this in Matthew 10:30. Psalm 56:8 MSG reads, "You've kept track of my every toss and turn through the sleepless nights, each tear entered in your ledger, each ache written in your book."

Reflection

Before we move on to the next chapter, let's reflect on and discuss what we've covered in this chapter:

1. After reading this chapter, what resonates with you?

2. Are you busy doing things to hide or mask a deeper issue?

3. Are you too busy and find it difficult to pause and unwind, to do nothing, to sit quietly and refresh? Be honest. Explain.

4. What will you do to become more attentive, conscious, and aware?

5. What have you learned that made you realize the need to establish boundaries in your life and relationships?

6. What are the areas in your life that weaken your resolve to maintain these boundaries? What are you doing to strengthen your resolve?

7. What was your most recent "Divine Notification?"

8. Did you 'silence' the "Divine Notification?" Why or why not?

"If you give up on the idea that your voice can make a difference, then other voices will fill the void."
—Barack Obama, 44th U.S. President

CHAPTER FIVE

Six Notes of Denial
No More Missed Moments

> *"You were born for a reason, created exactly as you are for a reason, for a special assignment that only you can fulfill. A time will come when you will be called. And it's a moment to celebrate, not a moment to be ashamed of."*
> —Nara Lee

It starts early in life—the urge to fit in. The pull to be like everyone else. The need to conform and blend into the crowd: don't stick out, and definitely don't be unique. Shame. Insecurity. Loneliness. Insecurity. Private battles. They all start early in life.

The denial starts early in life, as children.

It happened in 1974, but I didn't recall and filter the compelling lessons from it until 2017, when I was preparing to speak at a women's empowerment summit. I was asked to talk about "purpose." Now, this was over five years ago. As I began to pray and prepare my speech, a childhood memory came to mind. It was as if it'd been awakened in that moment—42 years later. I had completely put it out of my mind, and then it came flowing—not rushing—back to me.

Private Lessons, Private Battles

Six notes.

I don't know why I tucked the memory away, suppressed it somehow, but I did. And it was unearthed just when it needed to be—*for purpose, on purpose*. I used the "six notes" incident to speak about purpose.

I developed a love for music in the fourth grade. If you've ever been in the school band, you know the drill, but if you haven't, the first thing you should know is that band class starts with preparation.

Arriving early was one of the keys to success. You needed time to set up your instrument, retrieve the sheet music for the day, position your bandstand, warm up, and practice before the bandmaster stepped onto the platform. Preparation was everything. The activity in the band room was frenzied—sometimes rushed and always noisy—before the band director came in. After we'd been in the band room for a few minutes, you could hear us all over campus. Back then, the band room was not soundproof. You can imagine the loud blasts of warming up a trumpet or a trombone and the craziness of everybody playing something simultaneously but not together. The high sounds of the flutes, trumpets, and clarinets; the low sounds of the trombones; the beating of the drums; the crashing of the cymbals; and the warm sounds of the saxophones and French horns—so many noises from so many instruments.

The preparation period was chaos. There was no format, only the sound of each band member preparing in their own way. You were warming up your instrument, going through some drills, and making sure you knew your part. You didn't want to stand out because you missed some notes or because your instrument squeaked. It was loud and spontaneous, and in the end, we'd be ready when the bandmaster stepped onto the platform.

In bands and orchestras, there are first-, second-, and third-chair tiers based on skill, and it was competitive. Being the first chair is especially coveted as they hold the most power after the conductor, and the rest of the ensemble looks to the first chair for cues on musicality and performance. Because of this, the position of the first chair usually goes to an accomplished musician who is conscientious and mature enough to lead the section. The students who had the first three chairs defended the privilege by striving to be better than those students who challenged the seats. In our band, there was a challenge at least once a week. Whenever someone challenged the first chair, crucial moments determined victory or defeat.

I was the third-chair alto saxophonist. And I was determined to get to the second chair, though not the first because I didn't want the solos. I wanted to be one of the best, but I did not want to play alone.

Things came to a head when our band started preparing for the annual Florida State Band Competition. The band director asked me if I wanted to compete as the student conductor, and I said "yes". I was a choir director at my church, so it was a no-brainer. As the choir director and student conductor, my back was to the audience. *No one would be looking at my face.* I didn't have to look at or even think about the faces; I could just focus on the music.

Naturally, I was excited about being the student conductor.

I studied the composition and prepared myself. About a week later, the band director introduced the other pieces we were to perform at the competition. The unthinkable happened. In addition to directing a composition, I had a third chair solo, which went against everything in my mindset. The best singers sang the solo. The best musicians play the solo.

Nausea. Anxiety. Fear.

> "Step into your place and embrace your uniqueness. Your unique place in the world. Your purpose. Don't deny your gift, skill, talent, or commitment. Don't deny your story..."

I practiced at home as diligently as I'd always done, but each time I had to play the solo, my horn squeaked. I was worried that the same thing would happen when I played at the competition. I kept reminding myself that warming up my horn would take care of that. I tried to bolster my confidence. I didn't tell anyone how I was feeling.

I kept rehearsing and always warmed up my horn. The solo was simple—an allegro of six notes played alone as the entire band rested.

As the rehearsal went on, my anxiety increased. It's funny how we didn't use words like "anxiety" back then.

I played the six notes during rehearsals, nearly shaking with trepidation. I managed to play without squeaking, but I was so nervous every day.

I got a tiny splinter in my index finger, which was the finger I used to press the first note of the six notes. As you can imagine, my nerves skyrocketed. I focused so much on the splinter that you'd have thought I'd broken my finger. I even put a Band-Aid on it, hoping the band director would think I had a significant injury and decide to assign the solo to the first chair. He didn't. He couldn't. The composition's solo was strictly for the third chair—on purpose, I later learned. So a reassignment would likely have disqualified our band from the competition.

Then the day arrived—a sunny Florida morning. Our band was among hundreds of bands from all over the state, converging in Tallahassee for the school band finale.

I was nervous and eager to get it all over with. We watched from the audience as each band played its three compositions for the panel of judges. It was our turn, and the student conductor competition was the first piece. I took my place on the bandstand and confidently led the band through the music. We played our next piece, and then it was time for the finale—and my dreaded solo. I knew the notes. I'd prepared thoroughly. I prayed. I crossed my fingers.

Our band director started the composition, giving me a nod of encouragement. The auditorium was full of melodies.

Throughout the build-up to my solo part, I felt the anticipation, the confidence, and then, when the rhythm indicated it was time for the six notes, I…

I didn't play them!

I panicked. I lay my horn across my lap and put my head down!

The room was silent.

There was a void.

There was an absence of what should have filled that space.

In the single second before the first of the six notes were to fill the orchestra room, in front of the panel of judges, in front of my bandmates who knew my discipline as a musician, I put my head down and kept it down until what felt like a lifetime had passed. It was only six notes—tah-dah-dah-tah-dah-dah!

Those six notes were part of the musical composition that was one of our band's pieces for the competition and, thus, essential to our band's overall rating. We received an "Excellent" rating. Would we have received a "Superior" rating if the six notes were heard? Only God knows.

Not played. Missing. Void. Silence.

You can imagine what happened afterward. No one said a word to me or asked me, "What happened?" I think they all knew. What did I lose? I lost an opportunity to stand in my place. I dropped the ball. What would have happened if I'd played my role, my notes? I don't know; I learned from this incident and used that lesson at the empowerment summit. A missed middle school band moment traveled through time and served its purpose on another stage in 2017, as well as now. Who knew?

PLAYING THE "SIX NOTES"

Here's what I've learned from that incident.

1. The solo doesn't always go to the first chair—the most qualified, the highest ranking, the most visible, the most skilled, the one at the top of their game. Sometimes, the solo, the premium assignment, the prestige, the honor, the opportunity will come to you.

2. Prepare yourself: The lack of confidence can destroy an opportunity you're skilled and ready for.

3. Playing the "six notes" is not just about you but about the whole "band"—the whole, the team, the body, your family, your friends, your business, your local church, your next move.

4. Strive to be the best even as a "third chair." In any position—be it in your job, your career, a local ministry, volunteer work—give your all.

5. God will give you opportunities you do not feel qualified for.

6. God will open doors for you, and you must shut down fear, anxiety, low self-esteem, dislikes, internal wars, and everything that defeats your purpose.

7. Don't allow feeling a certain way about things or people—even yourself—keep you from experiencing a divine moment of your purpose and destiny.

8. Walk through the doors of opportunity with your head held high, knowing you prepared for this moment—play the six notes!

9. Step into the space prepared just for you.

10. Show up where you need to.

11. Complete your assignment, and don't be afraid of failing before you even play the first note—regret hides in the fear of risk and in the pursuit of perfection.

Don't allow a void to form in this world because you didn't play the "six notes."

Step into your place and embrace your uniqueness. Your unique place in the world. Your purpose. Don't deny your gift, skill, talent, or commitment. Don't deny your story. Don't deny your voice in the world. Standing out and speaking up take boldness and confidence—inner confidence. I'm not talking about arrogance or feigned confidence but inner confidence nurtured from the fact that you are enough and full of purpose.

We used to say "get in where you fit in" when several of us went to the drive-in movies in a two-seater. We contorted our bodies—young bodies, I must add—in ways that only very young people could. We twisted and bent our limbs out of their normal shapes just to fit in and get to the movie we wanted to see. That was then and for that time. Too many of us try and contort our bodies, beliefs, personalities, likes, and dislikes to fit what "they" like—*just to fit in.*

You can't afford to get in where you fit in and be out of alignment with your purpose. You don't have time to "fit in" within circles and groups that were not designed for you. You dumb yourself down to fit in. You scale down your dreams just to fit in. You feel uncomfortable because the space is not cultivated for you. You show up at places or events just to fit in. If you are not careful, you will contort yourself to fit into ungodly systems, unnecessary commitments, unfruitful and toxic relationships, and a system that denies God's Sovereignty and Purpose in your life.

Too often, we work too hard at trying to be "normal" instead of on being ourselves. Often, we think being normal will gain us acceptance, but, truth be told, you must accept yourself above all else and regardless of everybody else. Being acceptable to people will change throughout a lifetime. People will cheer for you one day and despise you the next; they will ignore you, write you off, pretend not to "see" you—the list is endless. But you are already accepted where it matters the most. You are accepted as the Beloved of God.

Reflection

Before we move on to the next chapter, let's reflect on and discuss what we've covered in this chapter:

1. Do you find yourself struggling with the private desire and longing to be accepted and affirmed by others? Be honest.

2. Are you contorting and twisting yourself to fit into a particular group? Be honest.

3. What opportunity have you missed? Did you drop the ball? What have you learned from it? Be honest.

4. What are you stepping back from because of the fear of failure or the need for perfection?

5. Thinking back to Chapter 2 and the words you used to describe yourself, which of them speak to your uniqueness and purpose?

6. Do you spend more time talking about what has not happened for you as expected or about what can happen for you? Explain. Be honest.

> "Always be yourself. At the end of the day, that's all you've really got; when you strip everything down, that's all you've got, so always be yourself."
> -Al Roker

...

"If every time there is a problem,
you think it is someone else then,
for heaven's sake, you could be the
problem. I'm not trying to
cause you to loathe yourself
but to ask, 'Is it I?'"

CHAPTER SIX

What to Do When the Problem Is You
Say Less

> *"The battles that count aren't the ones for gold medals. The struggles within yourself—the invisible, inevitable battles inside all of us—that's where it's at."*
> —Jesse Owens

Jesse Owens was a global champion, track and field athlete, ambassador, and businessman. He set world records in 1935 and won four gold medals in the 1936 Olympics. Yes…1936! Owens set Olympic records running the 100-meter event in 10.3 seconds, the 200-meter run in 20.7 seconds, the long jump in 26.4 feet, and the 4 × 100-meter relay in 39.8 seconds. When you read about his life, you come to understand that behind the glory is an incredible story. I like what Owens said: it's the invisible battles within us that are the hardest to fight and win. Each of us has our own struggles that are invisible to other people.

YOU COULD BE THE PROBLEM AND NOT KNOW IT

It's true that there are things we won't acknowledge. Sometimes, we are oblivious to the fact that we are the problem.

What does this have to do with hearing from God? Everything. Remember we talked about being open? Focusing on "being" instead of "doing"? Here's what I mean.

We know these battles, we're the only ones who can confront them, and only we can win them. And we can win them.

What do you do when the problem is looking back at you from the mirror? I faced the same question. It is so strange that we cannot acknowledge them easily or honestly. It is a process. I thought of Narcissus. In Greek mythology, Narcissus is a man who loves his appearance more than anything else. He misses opportunities, deep connections, and even a realistic view of life because he's too busy looking at himself and admiring his own image.

He's so in love with his own image that when he sees his reflection in a pool of water, he's transfixed to the point that he wastes away and dies. Till the very end, he can't see that he is the problem. I had to admit that I was the problem on numerous occasions—in business, relationships, finances, leadership, and, most importantly, my relationship with God. I had to admit that I was the problem when my self-esteem was at an all-time low and when I overestimated myself. Truth be told, I was in love with my own image, but I didn't even know myself. I had to get to know me. If I can't see myself as I am, I can't truly see God for His Authority, Power, and Lordship.

I am thankful to God for teaching me. I know every battle and lesson will not feel good or be easy to learn. Some made me cry long into the night. Some made me laugh. Some gave me the space to breathe and exhale with relief. Some shook me to the core. Many changed my mindset, agenda, and motive. Many made me set boundaries. Many humbled me. All of them have changed the way I live and will live the rest of my life.

> "One of the most important lessons in life is learning to recognize when you are the problem."

The definition of and common belief about the word "problem" literally send chills down the back of the average shift leader, supervisor, controller, parent, business owner, bank teller, and almost every person responsible for making things go right. The mere mention of the word raises red flags; it causes pink slips and dismissals, bankruptcy, litigations, alarms, uproars on social media, parent–teacher conferences, misfortune—the list goes on and on. But let's reframe how we view it. "Problem" also means an opportunity to drive solutions. It means a need can be met. It means illumination and enlightenment can come forth. It means rescue and healing can manifest. If there is a problem, there is a solution. As they say, "You're either part of the problem or part of the solution."

Once, when I was seven years old, I was outside with my mother, just playing around while she hung laundry on the clothesline behind our house. I remember that day so clearly; it was gorgeous outside, and a light wind was blowing the sheets in the breeze. The sky was a brilliant blue, and a few wisps of clouds were scattered about. I loved the sound of the sheets blowing in the wind, and after a few minutes of lying on the grass while looking up at the sky and imagining being able to fly, I got up, looking for something else to do. I'd made a few mud pies earlier that day.

I'd caught a dragonfly and put it in a jar after poking a couple of holes in the lid.

I took my trivial but common problem to my mom.

"I'm bored," I said.

She kept hanging laundry on the clothesline and, without looking, responded, "You make your own fun."

Bam. Just like that, I understood. My inner self fully grasped what my mother taught me that day. She didn't sugarcoat it; she didn't stop what she was doing to placate me, nor did she respond bitterly with "Get out of my face"—not that she ever did.

You make your own fun. That is the truth. Regardless of whether you're in a room full of people, the playground of your dreams, the job of your dreams, or the relationship of your dreams, you are central to any enjoyment you will ever have. Conversely, you are central to understanding and even solving many of the problems "you" will ever have. I didn't say *all* of the problems, but many of them. My bored seven-year-old self was looking outside for solutions to a problem I could solve. You won't believe me when I tell you I had siblings, cousins, and friends to play with, but I was still bored.

One of the most important lessons in life is learning to recognize when you are the problem.

"Is it I?" If you've read Matthew 26, you already know. It was a pivotal moment in the history of civilization, one never to be forgotten. Before His crucifixion, Jesus has the last supper with his disciples. He knew from the beginning—when he selected the twelve individuals, some three years before, to teach and impart the principles and teachings of the Kingdom of God—that one of them would betray Him to death. In fact, He knew about each of them. At the table that evening, Jesus makes it known that He knows who will betray Him and deliver Him for crucifixion.

> "And they were exceeding sorrowful, and began every one of them to say unto him, Lord, is it I?"
> —Matthew 26:22 KJV

On hearing Jesus, everyone at the table questions themselves. "Is it I?" and "Who is it?" hang heavy in the air. The elephant in the room is now loud and foreboding. We know it is Judas, and Judas knows it too. Judas's crime is unspeakable, and he sits at that table knowing full well what's in his heart and mind.

This may seem too severe of an example, but it is necessary to make this point. I can ask myself, "Is it I?" but it is far more difficult to answer with an astounding, confident, and authentic "Yes." Why is it so hard for us to ask deep questions and admit the answers honestly? For me, the issue was not having a clear view of who I am, denying some of my weaknesses, having tunnel vision, and being outwardly focused on doing something. The moment I recognized this and decided to let go of checking boxes was monumental.

Private Lessons, Private Battles

I'm not a therapist, psychologist, or counselor by any stretch of the imagination. I do know, however, that we play the blame game and tend to point the finger. I don't know who said it, but there's this saying that when we are pointing a finger at another, four other fingers are pointing back at us. But do you notice that those four fingers are tucked away tightly, almost out of view?

"They" are not always the problem. Maybe "they" are the people at your job. Your spouse. Your friends. Your parents. The people at church. The postal workers. The waitress. The valet. The cashiers. Your children. The teachers. The other drivers. Him. Her. Them.

If every time there is a problem, you think it is someone else—then, for heaven's sake, you could be the problem. I'm not trying to cause you to loathe yourself but to ask, "Is it I?" I know it's not easy, but it is necessary for alignment, resolve, growth, and inner peace. No more deflections, projections, cover-ups, or emotional denial—only the truth. . A hidden problem is still a problem. Status, leadership, wealth, rank, pedigree, influence—everyone needs to address their "problem." Denial doesn't change the truth.

> "Let a man examine himself."
> —1 Corinthians 11:28

Examine your heart, test your motives, and expose your inner thoughts on everything that matters. This should be at the top of your list of things to do for self-care. It is unconventional and often uncelebrated, but there is no shame in gaining clarity about the problem. The problem may lie in how you and I are showing up and interacting in the world; it could also concern how we are interacting with ourselves internally—by that, I mean our words to ourselves and about ourselves. I believe we have to recognize the need to resolve that which has remained unresolved in our souls and our hearts for far too long. Are there lessons intended for you to unearth in the long forgotten graveyard of unhealed emotions? We have to confront ourselves to reveal our best selves. So, would you admit how you feel right now about who you are and whatever you are facing right now, even if you don't have the answers? Beyond the filtered photos, laughs, makeovers, parties, and every other pretended perfection of life, who are you? It's not "them" right now; it's you. Don't be afraid to confront the inner struggle to become, to survive, to live, to thrive, to realize, and to face truths about yourself. Again, human nature is to look outside of ourselves to evaluate and judge the behavior, motives, successes, failures, and even words of others, but the truth is that we do not have the capacity, knowledge, or right to do any of that. God is the only one who can look inside of us and actually see and know the whole of our hearts. Inside, where the inner life—the private life—is going on. Inside, where life springs from the heart.

WHAT TO DO WHEN THE PROBLEM IS THAT YOU DISHONOR YOURSELF

"Deal with yourself as an individual worthy of respect and make everyone else deal with you the same way."
—Nikki Giovanni

Honor is defined as high respect and great esteem. Tell me, can we truly honor someone else without first honoring ourselves?

Honor yourself with boundaries—"yes" be "yes" and your "no" be "no." Honor yourself with love. I love the Word of God, and the following scripture reminds me to speak kind words to other people and to never forget to speak kind words to myself: "Kind words are like honey—sweet to the soul and healthy for the body" (Proverbs 16:24 NLV).

Self-care is a big money-making and marketing trend right now. There are books, bath bombs, spa days, themed trips, wines, "spiritual cleansing" rituals, clothing lines, social media platforms, and who knows what else purporting self-care. I love the spa, travel, long baths, and other things we do for our bodies. But we must give more self care attention to our inner selves--our souls, minds, and spirits. By the way, spiritual cleansing can only be achieved through Christ Jesus. We can dress it up as much as we want, but if the inner life, the private life, is a wreck, you will be crying in your car. You will be furious, frustrated, sad, still hateful, vengeful, and unfulfilled.

You don't need a lot of money to practice self-care. Self-care is soul-care, body-care, and mind-care. The first thing is to recognize who and whose you are and that no one is responsible for taking care of you but you—and God's got you. Extend yourself love, and then you can authentically extend it to everyone else. Extend yourself grace. Extend yourself honor. In all that you are laboring over, ask yourselves these two questions: Does this honor God? Does this honor me?

WHAT TO DO WHEN THE PROBLEM IS THAT YOU'RE FRUSTRATED

"Anger and frustration are the result of you not being authentic somewhere in your life or with someone in your life. Being fake about anything creates a block inside of you. Life can't work for you if you don't show up as you."
—Jason Mraz

Frustration is the feeling of being upset or annoyed, especially because of the inability to change or achieve something or to control something or someone. Think of a failed relationship, or even a good relationship, in which you are not giving your best but want everything. Or think of a job where you aren't bothering to perform well, instead coming in late, going to lunch early, or otherwise slacking off. Is the finger pointing at what "they" are doing or not doing? We cannot change anyone. Sometimes, I have trouble changing and controlling even myself. I've learned to be more focused on managing myself and not on trying to control other people.

WHAT TO DO WHEN THE PROBLEM IS THAT YOU FEEL INSECURE AND INADEQUATE

"The real difficulty is to overcome how you think about yourself."
—Maya Angelou

It could have started in kindergarten, on the kickball field, in middle school, with a relationship, on a job, or in a variety of situations. It could have started from the seeds of doubt and destruction your parents or others planted in you.

> You will never amount to anything.
> Everything you touch turns to sand.
> You are so destructive.
> You are my worst child.

Such words have been planted in people, and they later take root, grow, and spring up as insecurity, inadequacy, and even anger or resentment. Insecurity can be a short-term or a long-lasting feeling—the feeling that everyone is looking at you and waiting for you to trip, stumble, or fail in some way. Feeling insecure and inadequate can cause you to be awkward and uncomfortable everywhere, even in your own skin. One way to deal with these feelings is to correct how we see ourselves and how we feel about ourselves. One of the things I did was understand that the past is the past. Yesterday cannot be recovered or relived. The lies we listen to and the lies we tell ourselves can keep us stuck in feelings of insecurity and inadequacy.

You already possess what you need to be yourself in this world. Feelings don't necessarily signal truth; they can also be a response to a lie. No one else can compare to you, and vice versa. No comparisons. You have no idea, beyond what you see from a distance (or on social media), what other people are really doing or who they truly are.

If your feelings of inadequacy and insecurity stem from childhood experiences or from traumatic experiences you have endured or are enduring, know that you can overcome them to live more fully and peacefully, beginning today. Be aware of the emotions that are playing out in you because they affect everyone you meet and everything you do. Start purging yourself of negative words and start speaking truth to yourself. Capture your first thoughts in the morning and make sure you stop negative thinking at the beginning of your day. Work on feeling good in your own skin from the inside, not just looking good on the outside. Accept that you are already what you need to be to live your best life!

Carefully consider what Philippians 4:8–9 MSG tells us: "Summing it all up, friends, I'd say you'll do best by filling your minds and meditating on things true, noble, reputable, authentic, compelling, gracious—the best, not the worst; the beautiful, not the ugly; things to praise, not things to curse. Put into practice what you learned from me, what you heard and saw and realized. Do that, and God, who makes everything work together, will work you into His most excellent harmonies."

WHAT TO DO WHEN THE PROBLEM IS THAT YOU DUMB YOURSELF DOWN

I mentioned this earlier and it's worth revisiting. Dumbing yourself down means making yourself small, less intelligent, or less of who you are to gain someone or some appeal. Overestimating yourself means you still live outside of reality. God wants to bless you and use you for who you are, not who you pretend to be. The people you have dumbed yourself down for probably know it, but it is vital that you recognize it. Accept it and vow not to ever make yourself dumb and small just to make other people comfortable, to make them feel good at the expense of yourself, or to placate some void in your own self, like loneliness, insecurity, or the need for validation. It will never be fruitful, and you, my friend, will be hurt in the process. Dumbing yourself down will cause you to drift away from your real self and the purpose of your life. It makes you apathetic and emotionally dependent on other people for approval and validation. Dumbing yourself down inherently makes you feel small, insecure, inadequate, and knotted up inside. Let me be clear—dumbing yourself down is not false humility; it involves lowering your intelligence and pretending to be someone you are not just to get into "the circle," certain rooms, or a relationship. It means you are denying your origin and your purpose. God carefully crafted you with respect, honor, and reverence. You are wonderfully made by God, our Creator. That's your origin. By dumbing yourself down, you are elevating other people over God's divine purpose. Again, wants to bless you and use you for who you are, not who you pretend to be.

Overestimating yourself is also dangerous and diminishing. Denial is the enemy of your soul and your destiny.

Live your life and practice being the best version (the divinely designed unique version, not the fashion-labeled and trend-following version) of you at every table and in every room. If you are not being real and authentic, you will not be able to discern your place there. We are often pushed to find a table and take a seat. In fact, we are often told to push our way to the table and ensure we have a seat. Think about this in terms of your life, and then decide if you want a seat at "the table." Not all tables are for you. That doesn't mean all tables are bad, simply that not all of them are for you. Don't just find a seat anywhere—not all seats are for you. Don't get caught up in the rat race for fame, position, pseudo-influence, approval, validation, or any of those "out-of-body" experiences. I say "out-of-body" experiences because if they are not in alignment with who you are—who God wants you to be—it will be an epic failure. *Actualize your inner self, guided by God's Word instead of feelings, emotions, or external influences.*

Remember, the LORD will prepare a table for you in full view of your enemies. If He will do it in front of your enemies, it will be done in full view of anyone else at the table as well.

Be yourself and stand firm in who you are. Sit at God's table, and then you will be able to discern the other tables where you have an assigned seat. Whether they fight you over your assigned seat or not, it is your seat. Sit down.

WHAT TO DO WHEN THE PROBLEM IS THAT YOU ARE TOO RELIGIOUS

I seriously considered leaving this out, but I can't. Being too religious is a thing. Over the years, I've heard people say, "Some folks are so holy that they are no earthly good." I want to start a campaign to replace that statement with "Some folks are so religious that they are not holy and no earthly good for the Kingdom!" The truth is that, sometimes, what we put forth as holy are religion and religious rituals. Sometimes, we are practicing religion, as I talked about in a previous chapter. It can be a slippery slope; you may fall into religion and neglect true relationship with

God. This is why our private practice is so vital.

I think about Le'Andria Johnson's 2011 album entitled The *Awakening of Le'Andria Johnson*. She won a Grammy award for the song "Jesus." You can look up the full version of the song, but here is the first and last line of the song:

> "Look at myself in the mirror
> Religion look'in back at me
> I threw my hands in the air and the law arrested me.
> But I'm in my closet
> Yes I am
> I'm in my closet
> Time after time
> Praying Jesus, singing Jesus, crying Jesus."

When you don't feel like anyone can hear you, much less the Sovereign God and Creator of all creation, remember He hears you. Not only does He hear you, but He also sees you, and He wants you to know it. Not only does He see you and hear you, but He feels you. God is doing something in you that only He can explain, but you will benefit. Jesus is our intercessor, and He sacrificed his life for our salvation, redemption, healing, and benefit. I can't help but remember 3 John 1:2 KJV: "Beloved, I wish above all things that you prosper and be in good health, even as your soul prospers." That means our whole self. God wants us to be whole. He wants us to welcome Him into every area of our lives. He wants us to be open and honest about it all, which makes perfect sense because He already knows every detail—spoken and unspoken, admitted and unadmitted.

Reflection

Before we move on to the next chapter, let's reflect on and discuss what we've covered in this chapter:

1. How have you dishonored yourself in the past? Explain.

2. Are you or have you been frustrated with people for not supporting you? Explain.

3. Are you more critical of others and less critical of yourself? Why?

4. What comes to your mind when considering the possibility that you may have dumbed yourself down in some situations? Be honest.

5. How will this chapter impact your prayer life going forward?

6. What do you now recognize and release from having read this chapter?

7. What does God's mercy and grace have to do with your ability to admit when you're wrong?

8. Sometimes situations and people trigger negativity in us; what/who have you recognized as triggers in your life and how will you now respond?

"Although we do not use actual weapons, we must employ spiritual weapons. We must wear spiritual armor in all cases and at all times."

CHAPTER SEVEN

Battle-Tested Lessons
Experienced, Toughened, Seasoned

"If you know the enemy and know yourself, you need not fear the result of a hundred battles."
—Sun Tzu, The Art of War

You are here. You are alive. Whether you categorize your struggle as small or Goliath, it's a battle. You are battle-tested at some level.

In the last chapter, we talked about what to do when the problem is you. That's a part of it all, and a very big part at that. But there are also times when you are not the problem but are central to the process of being battle-tested in your faith and your spiritual maturity. What does battle-tested mean? The Merriam-Webster dictionary defines it as "shown to be reliable and effective by being used in war" and "having experienced and been toughened by battle."

I have friends who are combat veterans. They have been deployed multiple times, experiencing battles and war at a level that others cannot imagine. They are battle-tested. They are reliable and effective witnesses—trained in warfare and alive to talk about it. They have been affected by it, and many wounds are not detectable to the human eye. But praise God, for He has all the information and is the Healer.

I, like many veterans, did not see combat. During my twenty years on active duty, I got really close to deploying a few times but didn't get off the tarmac. I can talk about the military on many levels, but I cannot speak as an eyewitness to combat. However, I can speak as an eyewitness to spiritual warfare. Now this may seem too broad a comparison, but this is how we must think about it. We are actually in spiritual combat—right now and for as long as we are alive on this earth. It's time we realize it.

Sun Tzu was a Chinese military strategist, writer, and philosopher, believed to have lived in the sixth century. His work resonates with me in many ways. As a retired military officer, I still remember reading this book while on active duty and seeing how much of it seems to have been taken from the holy scriptures and adapted. "If you know the enemy and know yourself, you need not fear the result of a hundred battles, "Tzu wrote.

> "Blessed be the LORD, my rock, who trains my hands for war, and
> my fingers for battle; he is my steadfast love and my fortress,
> my stronghold and my deliverer, my shield
> and he in whom I take refuge."
> —Psalm 144:1 NLT

We are engaged in a lifelong spiritual battle. I believe we often downplay and omit the seriousness of this type of warfare because of the distractions, rush, culture, and world systems that are anti-

God. We know the enemy. Ephesians 6:12 NLT tells us, "For we are not fighting against flesh-and-blood enemies, but against evil rulers and authorities of the unseen world, against mighty powers in this dark world, and against evil spirits in the heavenly places."

Although we do not use actual weapons, we must employ spiritual weapons. We must wear spiritual armor in all cases and at all times. The instructions for this can be found in Ephesians 6, as Paul the Apostle is clear about what we are engaged in and warns us to use the Armor of God. Verse 13 AMP reads:

"Therefore, put on the complete armor of God, so that you will be able to [successfully] resist and stand your ground in the evil day [of danger], and having done everything [that the crisis demands], to stand firm [in your place, fully prepared, immovable, victorious]."

I believe He speaks to us before, throughout, and after the battle. We have this confidence that we are not alone. These are the times we incline our hearing or, as someone shared with me the other day, position our antenna—we setting our station to Jesus to hear from Him. Then we must honor His voice above all others. The LORD is not sleeping through the seasons of our lives. He has already been where we are going. Our life on this earth has a beginning and an ending. He has been here. He is the artist who designed and curated the same stars, sun, and sky my ancestors gazed at and you and I see today. He is the Ancient of Days. He is the Alpha and the Omega.

We must honor His voice. While the antenna may be set to Jesus, we cannot allow ourselves to just "hear" without listening. I'm

> "I believe He speaks to us before, throughout, and after the battle. We have this confidence that we are not alone."

not saying you need an absolute quiet space to hear from God, not at all. You can be on a crowded bus and hear His voice. You can be anywhere, anytime and hear Him. That is one of the many beauties of our LORD. He is omnipresent, omniscient, and omnipotent. What I want to impress upon you is unexplainable in a sense. But please spend some quiet time, at the start of your day and throughout; this time you spend in the presence of God is unequaled. You don't have to say anything. Just take a posture of worship. His voice will amplify the silence. Surrender to His voice. He gives us inner strength and courage and always causes us to triumph.

In the military, we had guidance, regulations, and manuals for everything. For every event, mission, exercise, deployment, and battle, we had guidance. The regulation was the authority and was not open to individual interpretation. So why is it that we want to self-interpret God's authority in His word? As Jesus tells the devil in the wilderness, "No! The Scriptures say, 'People do not live by bread alone, but by every word that comes from the mouth of God'" (Matthew 4:4 NLT). We must not ever attempt to downplay, self-interpret, or deny the authority of God's word for we need His word more than we need breath. The Bible is not a directive of dos and don'ts, but for life. His Word is a lamp unto our feet and a light unto our paths, as written in Psalm 119:105. The Word of God will sustain us through every hill, every valley, and every battle. It is actually the Word of God that is the lesson.

CHOOSE YOUR BATTLES

In the military—in every unit I was assigned, which included two in foreign countries—we communicated in the same way. We used acronyms and said things like. "I got your six," "Headed to the TOC," "Roger that," "I'm tracking," and "Standby." Something else we would say was "Choose your battles." It's been many years since I retired, but to this day, I subscribe to the practice of choosing my battles. I've added "Let God be God" to the list now.

Choosing your battles is the strategy of only giving attention, energy, and responses to someone or something that matters. Choosing your battles is the pivotal point of knowing when to escalate or when to turn away. It is not solely a matter of winning or losing. You could win, but is it worth your time, reputation, energy, or attention? You could lose, but does it really matter in the grand scheme of things? Fighting every battle means you will be busy and exhausted with everything, leaving you without the energy or focus to fight the battles that matter.

THE BATTLE IS THE LORD'S

Choosing your battles is a daily exercise. It is tricky, sometimes unnerving, but necessary. 1 Chronicles 20:17 NIV reads, "You will not have to fight this battle. Take up your positions; stand firm and see the deliverance the LORD will give you, Judah, and Jerusalem. Do not be afraid; do not be discouraged. Go out to face them tomorrow, and the LORD will be with you."

In the Message, 1 Peter 4:12–15 says, "Friends, when life gets really difficult, don't jump to the conclusion that God isn't on the job. Instead, be glad that you are in the very thick of what Christ experienced. This is a spiritual refining process, with glory just around the corner. If you're abused because of Christ, count yourself fortunate. It's the Spirit of God and His glory in you that brought you to the notice of others."

Save your energy, strategies, and resources to build and uphold your faith. Don't forget that God will make things right.

Proverbs 20:22 MSG says, "Don't ever say, 'I'll get you for that!' Wait for God; He'll settle the score."

DECISIONS TO STAND

"Take up your positions; stand firm and see the deliverance the LORD will give you."

The enemy, the devil, uses the strategy of shooting arrows of lies to get you to believe him instead of the truth. Lies about yourself. Lies about your origin. Lies that you are all alone. Lies that God does not love you as He says. Lies about your value. Lies about relationships. Lies about faith. Lies about religion. Lies about everything. Don't spend even a minute going back and forth; instead, intentionally apply the battle strategy Jesus executed flawlessly when the devil came to Him in the wilderness.

Matthew 4 is where we can read it. Jesus is led by the Spirit into the wilderness to fast for forty days and forty nights, and afterward,

He is naturally famished. What happens next? The devil shows up with lies—lies that twist the Word of God. Jesus doesn't go back and forth with the devil. Being hungry, He heads out for bread and fish. He doesn't spend days, weeks, or years arguing with the devil over lies. He applies the Word of God. This is the strategy we must know and use to stand our ground. We have a true and solid foundation on which we stand—we need to know it.

I love this hymn, which was written by Edward Mote in 1834, because it so clearly describes where we stand:

> My hope is built on nothing less than Jesus's blood and righteousness; I dare not trust the sweetest frame,
> But wholly lean on Jesus's name.
> On Christ, the solid Rock, I stand.
> All other ground is sinking sand,
> All other ground is sinking sand.
> When darkness veils His lovely face,
> I rest on His unchanging grace.
> In every high and stormy gale,
> My anchor holds within the veil.
> His oath, His covenant, His blood
> Support me in the whelming flood.
> When all around my soul gives way,
> He then is all my hope and stay.
> When He shall come with trumpet sound,
> Oh, may I then in Him be found;
> Dressed in His righteousness alone,
> Faultless to stand before the throne.
> *Public Domain*

LEARNING TO RESPOND

Wouldn't it be fantastic if, when we were born, we were given a full comprehensive file that told us exactly how to live our lives? A file with photos and information for every day, every problem, every issue, and every decision?

It is interesting what I discovered on the final day of writing this chapter. I woke up that morning feeling a bit of angst—for no reason, really. I planned to go for a morning walk, only to be distracted, but I ended up outside in my happy place, listening to the beautiful sounds of nature and thinking. Some negative thoughts creeped in, so I got up and just walked around the yard. But I kept having negative thoughts. I shifted my thoughts to this phrase: "Start fresh, living your life well."

I walked back to the yard and decided to just read some scriptural passages to shift my thinking. Reading the Bible does more than we can comprehend or explain, but clearly Divine Notifications are the byproduct of getting into the Word. "Thy Word is a lamp unto my feet and a light unto my path." Psalm 119:105 KJV

I sat down outside and decided to just open the Bible and read from wherever it opened. It opened to Ecclesiastes 12 MSG. My eyes landed on verses 6–7: "Life, lovely while it lasts, is soon over. Life as we know it, precious and beautiful, ends. The body is put back in the same ground it came from. The spirit returns to God, who first breathed it."

I had one of those moments where I paused, looked up, and said, "LORD, are you talking to me?" Returning to the page, my eyes landed on verses 9–14, subtitled "The Final Word": "Besides being wise himself, the Quester (King Solomon) also taught others knowledge. He weighed, examined, and arranged many proverbs. The Quester did his best to find the right words and write the plain truth. The words of the wise prod us to live well. They're like nails hammered home, holding life together. They are given by God, the one Shepherd. But regarding anything beyond this, dear friend, go easy. There's no end to the publishing of books, and constant study wears you out so you're no good for anything else. The last and final word is this: Fear God. Do what he tells you. And that's it. Eventually God will bring everything that we do out into the open and judge it according to its hidden intent, whether it's good or evil."

Some of us are living in the now, while some are living in the past, but we cannot live in the future. We can only hope for it and live divinely in it when it comes. We can hope to live by God's design only when we learn how to respond to life, regardless of the turns it takes. I do not pretend here that I will always respond perfectly in the moment, but what I am learning is that a response with divine knowledge is the best response. I can choose to reset. I can choose to refresh. I can choose to restart. All three are needed at one time or another. Life has a way of dumbfounding us, literally taking our breath away at times and making us feel like lying down, running away, or just quitting—because unwanted things happened or because of disappointment about what didn't happen—at other times.

Making sense of it all is impossible, but our responses determine a lot of things. Through experience and personal growth, we become more aware and conscious of our power to choose how we respond. And in all of it allowing God to demonstrate His love, grace, and promises.

Reflection

Before we move on to the next chapter, let's reflect on and discuss what we've covered in this chapter:

1. In which areas of your life have you been battle-tested more than in others? Explain.

2. Are you at a point of resetting, refreshing, and restarting?

3. Name a life event you did not respond well to. How would you respond now? Does this response show growth and maturity?

4. What does James 1:2–4 mean to you going forward?

5. What would you share with a friend to help them overcome doubt, guilt, and selfishness?

"Unless we form the habit of going to the Bible in bright moments as well as in trouble, we cannot fully respond to its consolations because we lack equilibrium between light and darkness."
-Helen Keller

"Then Hagar called the Lord El Roi when He spoke to her, meaning: You are God Who Sees. "I'm out here in this wilderness still living after seeing Him who sees me with understanding and compassion."

God never sleeps, He sees, He is aware, He is the great Omnipresent God."
-Genesis 16:13 AMP, Paraphrased

PART II
GOD NOTICES YOU

"It is important to note that God is the Sovereign LORD, and He speaks anytime, anywhere, and anyway He wants to..."

CHAPTER EIGHT

Moses: Quiet Loudness
God Is Still Speaking

Everything Speaks. Even silence can speak volumes.

The life lessons of Moses cannot be detailed in this short chapter. You can read about him in Exodus 2 and other scriptures, including Hebrews 11:23–29. Moses was born in Egypt during time the Jewish people were enslaved. His parents were of the highly regarded tribe of Levi. They already had two other children, Miriam and Aaron, when Moses was born.

Still, allow me to break it down into a very brief summary.

In Act I, we see how Moses's mother hides him in a basket and sets it afloat on the Nile River in an attempt to save him from the king's decree to murder every Jewish newborn boy. The daughter of the pharaoh notices the basket, and Moses is adopted and brought up as royalty, in an environment of wealth, culture, extensive education, and influence.

PRIVATE LESSONS, PRIVATE BATTLES

In Act II, several events happen in quick succession. Moses becomes a fugitive on the run after murdering an Egyptian man and hiding the body in a shallow grave. We are privy to Moses's thoughts about the crime when he realizes somebody saw what he did. He flees to avoid prosecution and the death penalty that is sure to follow.

> "God uses his curiosity to launch Moses into his divine destiny—leading the Jews out of slavery."

In Act III, Moses is living in a different country, with new relationships, a new family, and a very different occupation. His past is behind him, and he has an entirely new focus. He works in a wide-open terrain as a shepherd.

To contextualize this brief summary, you should know Moses is about forty years old when he flees to a place over six thousand miles away, called Midian. He works for his father-in-law as a sheepherder at the "backside of the desert" for about another forty years.

This brings us to the point of this chapter. I will call it Act IV for consistency and brevity.

As recorded in Exodus 3:1–6 MSG, here's what unexpectedly happens to Moses one day:

He led the flock to the west end of the wilderness and came to the mountain of God, Horeb. The angel of GOD appeared to him in flames of fire blazing out of the middle of a bush. He looked. The bush was blazing away but it didn't burn up. Moses said, "What's going on here? I can't believe this! Amazing! Why doesn't the bush burn up?" GOD saw that he had stopped to look. God called to him from out of the bush, "Moses! Moses!"

It is important to note that God is the Sovereign LORD, and He speaks anytime, anywhere, and anyway He wants to. He spoke to Moses in an unusual way, right?

Moses said, "Yes? I'm right here!" God said, "Don't come any closer. Remove your sandals from your feet. You're standing on holy ground." Then he said, "I am the God of your father: The God of Abraham, the God of Isaac, the God of Jacob."

Are we talking about the same person? Yes. Moses notices, and God reveals Himself to him in an unprecedented way.

Nothing spectacular or interesting was happening prior to this incident. Moses was walking about as he'd done numerous times before, looking around vigilantly to guard against wolves and other dangers. However, Moses doesn't just keep walking, instead drawing closer to better see the odd phenomenon. God uses his curiosity to launch Moses into his divine destiny—leading the Jews out of slavery. The bush is the catalyst for drawing him into the presence of God. What are you missing and disregarding in your life? Take the time to "see" what is around you. *Never confuse awareness with sensitivity.*

"We have to believe we can reach God, and we must have faith that He wants us. Our most valuable lessons are learned from our inner life."

CHAPTER NINE

Devotion: Private Practice
Undeniable Results

"Prayer enables us first inwardly to overcome the enemy and then outwardly to deal with him."
-Watchman Nee

Devotion is amazing, and I want to highlight two people who show us some astonishing facets of life, faith, pain, and devotion: Hannah and Cornelius. They are two different people living in different times. Hannah is introduced in the Old Testament, while Cornelius is introduced in the New Testament.

Hannah is a beautiful sister wife who is unable to conceive a child. She is bullied, badgered, and oppressed by Peninnah—who has no problem whatsoever conceiving, instead "spitting them out," as my grandmother may have said. Hannah is sad, grieved, and hurting, filled with immense personal pain. A pain no one can understand, not even her husband. A pain so deep that she stops eating. Year after year, Peninnah shames and provokes Hannah. Even when they visit the temple or church, Peninnah aggressively and spitefully hurts Hannah. Long story short (you must read it in 1 Samuel 1), Hannah is literally pushed to the breaking point. She responds with prayer. 1 Samuel 1:13 gives us a vivid picture of the scene inside the temple in those crucial moments. Hannah is on the altar, crying and praying. The Bible says, "She spoke in her heart; only her lips moved, but her voice was not heard." Eli, the priest, is in the temple, and when he sees Hannah, he actually thinks she's drunk. Of course, she isn't drunk in the way he thinks, though perhaps she is drunk on passionate prayer. God hears her voice. Neither Eli nor anyone else hears what she prays to God.

Hannah explains herself to Eli, telling him she's not drunk: "No, my lord, I am a woman of a sorrowful spirit."

Eli answers, "Go in peace: and the God of Israel grant thee thy petition that thou hast asked of him." 1 Samuel 1:17 KJV

Hannah stands up from the altar a changed woman. People see it on her face, and she starts eating again. She has her first child, and there is so much more ahead for her. God sees her. God hears her. God feels her. God blesses her.

Cornelius is a military officer with a reverence for God and a policy of doing what is right. He gives generously to people and prays consistently. What happens to him is stunning.

Here's Acts 10:3-4 ESV: "About the ninth hour of the day, he saw clearly in a vision an angel of God come in and say to him, 'Cornelius', And he stared at him in terror and said, 'What is it, Lord?'" The angel tells Cornelius to send some of his men to Joppa, where Simon Peter is staying in the home of Simon. He is to ask Peter to come to him at Caesarea. Cornelius responds and sends three of his men to Joppa.

Jumping ahead a few verses, here is what happens: God has been speaking to Peter, and when Cornelius's messengers arrive, Peter knows he must go with them to Cornelius's home in Caesarea just as the angel said. When they arrive, they find a gathering of expectant family and friends. When Cornelius sees Peter, he bows to his feet and worships him. Peter stops him and asks him why he has been summoned. Cornelius repeats his story about the angel and then asks Peter to share what God told him to say to them. Peter tells them about Jesus Christ, and while he is still speaking, the Holy Spirit falls upon Cornelius, his family, and friends, and they begin speaking in tongues and praising God.

> **"Hannah, Cornelius, you, and I—we have the ability to reach God..."**

This is amazing. Though Cornelius and the others had not heard the gospel of Jesus Christ, God sees Cornelius's practices of praying, sacrificing, giving, and serving. His heart is sincere, and he doesn't go unnoticed.

Hannah, Cornelius, you, and i—we have the ability to reach God. We have to believe we can reach God, and we must have faith that He wants us. Our most valuable lessons are learned from our inner life. Trusting God has undeniable results.

"Jacob realizes an awareness of God that he didn't know he possessed. He was aware of God's presence but didn't know it. From that moment on, he is open to a deeper awareness of God."

CHAPTER TEN

Jacob: The Power of Noticing
Alone Time

"Time alone in quiet solitude produces a deeper awareness, clarity, and inner strength."

Jacob, like each of us, has some issues. He was Isaac and Rebecca's son, and his brother is Esau. Jacob had a troubled past, filled with deception, both inner and outwardly, and was moving forward in the way that we all attempt to do; however, God providentially sets up an encounter with Jacob to allow him to really move on with peace and confidence for the days and years ahead of him and his descendants. Jacob was able to move on to his divinely designed destiny. Sometimes our past seems to threaten our future, but God wants us to move forward.

Esau and Jacob are two brothers divided and estranged because of deception, impulsiveness, and confused values. And sometimes, their home environment is a divided place too as their parents have different views about family, legacy, inheritance, fairness, and many other issues. Yet, they are people who revere God.

Like us, each of them has to find their way and their faith in God. Genesis 28:10–17 shows us Jacob after he left Beersheba and

> "You and I have the same access to the God of Heaven."

went to Haran: "He came to a certain place and camped for the night since the sun had set. He took one of the stones there, set it under his head and lay down to sleep. And he dreamed: A stairway was set on the ground, and it reached all the way to the sky; angels of God were going up and going down on it. Then God was right before him, saying, 'I am God, the God of Abraham your father and the God of Isaac. I'm giving the ground on which you are sleeping to you and to your descendants. Your descendants will be as the dust of the Earth; they'll stretch from west to east and from north to south. All the families of the Earth will bless themselves in you and your descendants. Yes. I'll stay with you, I'll protect you wherever you go, and I'll bring you back to this very ground. I'll stick with you until I've done everything I promised you.' Jacob woke up from his sleep. He said, 'God is in this place—truly. And I didn't even know it!' He was terrified. He whispered in awe, 'Incredible. Wonderful. Holy. This is God's House. This is the Gate of Heaven.'"

Awesome is loud, but awe is quiet. Jacob's response is not unusual, is it? Imagine dreaming about a stairway looming all the way over the clouds and horizon, connecting heaven and earth in a literal way! Then, seeing angels traveling up and down the stairway—like a road between heaven and earth! It doesn't end with his vision of the stairway; God speaks to him. As you trace back in the scriptures, you will remember that God speaks to Jacob's father Isaac in his quiet moments and to Abraham (Abram) on several occasions. He speaks to each of them, separately and privately, about themselves, their families, and what He has in store for them.

You and I have the same access to the God of heaven.

Jacob realizes an awareness of God that he didn't know he possessed. He was aware of God's presence but didn't know it. From that moment on, he is open to a deeper awareness of God.

"What can you do when the problem is you? Admit you are the problem. Admit you sinned. Admit you gossip. Admit you are self-centered and arrogant. Finally, change and turn away from it."

CHAPTER ELEVEN

David: When the Problem Is You

Own It

"Denial is dangerous yet each of us have been in denial at least once without even knowing it. We have to be humbly on guard."

The lady is guilty. She cannot cover it up or hide at this point. There are many witnesses. However, the man is also guilty. But in this situation, the guilty man (privately knowing he is guilty), on hearing of another man's guilt, failure, deception, and cruelty, condemns him as if he himself is perfect. He condemns the other guilty man publicly but privately has his own secrets.

As he is speaking and giving his opinion about the appropriate punishment for someone else who has committed an evil deed, the pendulum swings back in his direction—and stops.

The lady is Bathsheba. The highly opinionated guilty man is King David.

This story reads like a modern-day movie script because the issues are as old as mankind.

PRIVATE LESSONS, PRIVATE BATTLES

David has an affair with Bathsheba, she gets pregnant, and he plots to kill her husband. As commander in chief, he issues an order to make sure Bathsheba's husband stays on the front lines and is killed in action.

God Almighty sees every person, and He notices us when we don't want to be noticed. He sends Nathan, the prophet, to confront David. This is detailed in 2 Samuel 12.

Nathan shares the story of two men, one rich and the other poor, who live in the same town. The rich man has a sprawling ranch with herds of animals, while the poor man has just one little female lamb. The poor man and his family treat the lamb as a member of the family. One day the rich man has a dinner for an out-of-town guest but instead of taking from his herd, he takes the poor man's lamb to serve as the main course.

Nathan probably hopes and prays that David will see himself in the story so that he can say less. I imagine Nathan thought, "Surely, he can see himself in this scenario?"

David doesn't. In fact, the opposite occurs. When David hears the story, it triggers immediate anger and outrage: "The rich man who did this should be executed!"

David is justifiably angry at the injustice, but when Nathan says, "You are the man!" there is an immediate and profound response. Nathan doesn't stop there but gives David a message from God.

David accepts and acknowledges his brutal crime and cover up, disobedience, dishonor, lack of compassion, deception, cruelty—his sins.

What can you do when the problem is you? Admit you are the problem. Admit you sinned. Admit you gossip. Admit you are self-centered and arrogant. Finally, change and turn away from it. This situation and countless others reveal how evil, irreverent, self-centered, and self-righteous the best of us can be.

> "God Almighty sees every person, and He notices us when we don't want to be noticed."

David admits, "The problem is me." Psalm 51 NLT tells us what he said to the God of Heaven:

> 1 Have mercy on me, O God,
> because of your unfailing love.
> Because of your great compassion,
> blot out the stain of my sins.
>
> 2 Wash me clean from my guilt.
> Purify me from my sin.
>
> 3 For I recognize my rebellion;
> it haunts me day and night.
>
> 4 Against you, and you alone, have I sinned;
> I have done what is evil in your sight.
> You will be proved right in what you say,
> and your judgment against me is just.

5 For I was born a sinner—
yes, from the moment my mother conceived me.

6 But you desire honesty from the womb,
teaching me wisdom even there.

7 Purify me from my sins, and I will be clean;
wash me, and I will be whiter than snow.

8 Oh, give me back my joy again;
you have broken me—
now let me rejoice.

9 Don't keep looking at my sins.
Remove the stain of my guilt.

10 Create in me a clean heart, O God.
Renew a loyal spirit within me.

11 Do not banish me from your presence,
and don't take your Holy Spirit from me.

12 Restore to me the joy of your salvation,
and make me willing to obey you.

13 Then I will teach your ways to rebels,
and they will return to you.

14 Forgive me for shedding blood, O God who saves;
then I will joyfully sing of your forgiveness.

15 Unseal my lips, O Lord,
that my mouth may praise you.

16 You do not desire a sacrifice, or I would offer one.
You do not want a burnt offering.

17 The sacrifice you desire is a broken spirit.
You will not reject a broken and repentant heart, O God.

18 Look with favor on Zion and help her;
rebuild the walls of Jerusalem.

19 Then you will be pleased with sacrifices offered in the right spirit—with burnt offerings and whole burnt offerings. Then bulls will again be sacrificed on your altar.

"We do not want to be deceived, by ourselves or any other person, into believing a lie rather than the truth to satisfy our emotions, desires, and plans."

CHAPTER TWELVE

Thinking About It
Words to Live By

"Study this Book of Instruction continually. Meditate on it day and night so you will be sure to obey everything written in it. Only then will you prosper and succeed in all you do." Joshua 1:8 NLT

I pray you have found clarity and inner strength to make sense of life by deriving meaning from everyday experiences. You are on point when you see and hear clear lessons and receive divine inspiration in the common and simple things of life. God created us for this human experience, and He wants to be totally and completely involved in our lives—it's our choice, but in the end each of us will answer to our choice.

Let me leave a word of caution with you. In a world of shifting thoughts, faithlessness, arrogance, dark systems, false information and manipulation, ungodly trends, pretentious godliness, and false beliefs—every last one of us must be solidly and firmly planted in God's Word as the highest truth and premier authority.

2 Timothy 4:3 NLT says, "for a time is coming when people will no longer listen to sound and wholesome teaching. They will follow

> "God's Word as the highest truth and premier authority."

their own desires and will look for teachers who will tell them whatever their itching ears want to hear." These *people* could include you and me if we are not heeding God's Word and following His agenda. We do not want to be deceived, by ourselves or any other person, into believing a lie rather than the truth to satisfy our emotions, desires, and plans.

Let these scriptures be words to live by:

GOD HEARS YOU...

2 Samuel 22:7 ESV

In my distress, I called upon the Lord; to my God, I called. From His temple, he heard my voice, and my cry came to his ears.

Psalm 4:3 ESV

But know that the LORD has set apart the godly for Himself; the Lord hears when I call to Him.

Psalm 17:6 ESV

I call upon You, for You will answer me, O God; incline Your ear to me; hear my words.

Psalm 34:17 ESV

When the righteous cry for help, the LORD hears and delivers them out of all their troubles.

Psalm 28:7–8 NIV

Praise be to the LORD, for He has heard my cry for mercy. The LORD is my strength and my shield; my heart trusts in Him, and He helps me. My heart leaps for joy, and with my song I praise him.

Psalm 61:5 ESV

For You, O God, have heard my vows; You have given me the heritage of those who fear Your name.

Psalm 66:17–20 ESV

I cried to Him with my mouth, and high praise was on my tongue. If I had cherished iniquity in my heart, the LORD would not have listened. But truly God has listened; He has attended to the voice of my prayer. Blessed be God because he has not rejected my prayer or removed His steadfast love from me!

Psalm 77:1 ESV

I cry aloud to God, aloud to God, and He will hear me.

Psalm 84:8 ESV

O LORD God of hosts, hear my prayer; give ear, O God of Jacob! Selah

Psalm 139:4 ESV

Even before a word is on my tongue, behold, O Lord, you know it altogether.

Proverbs 15:29 ESV

The LORD is far from the wicked, but He hears the prayer of the righteous.

John 9:31 ESV

We know that God does not listen to sinners, but if anyone is a worshiper of God and does His will, God listens to him.

John 11:41–42 ESV

So they took away the stone. And Jesus lifted up His eyes and said, "Father, I thank You that You have heard Me. I knew that You always hear Me, but I said this on account of the people standing around, that they may believe that You sent Me."

1 Peter 3:12 ESV

For the eyes of the LORD are on the righteous, and His ears are open to their prayer. But the face of the LORD is against those who do evil.

1 John 5:14 ESV

And this is the confidence that we have toward Him, that if we ask anything according to His will He hears us.

GOD WHO SEES YOU...

Genesis 16:13 NIV

She gave this name to the LORD who spoke to her: "You are the God who sees me," for she said, "I have now seen the One who sees me."

Proverbs 15:3 NIV

The eyes of the LORD are everywhere, keeping watch on the wicked and the good.

Jeremiah 12:3a ESV

But you, O LORD, know me; You see Me, and test my heart toward You.

Psalm 33:18 NIV

But the eyes of the LORD are on those who fear Him, on those whose hope is in His unfailing love.

Jeremiah 1:5a ESV

Before I formed you in the womb, I knew you, and before you were born, I consecrated you.

2 Chronicles 16:9a NLT

The eyes of the LORD search the whole earth in order to strengthen those whose hearts are fully committed to him.

GOD FEELS YOU...

Genesis 1:26–28 AMP

God said, "Let Us [Father, Son, and Holy Spirit] make mankind in Our image, after Our likeness, and let them have complete authority over the fish of the sea, the birds of the air, the [tame] beasts, and over all of the earth, and over everything that creeps upon the earth." So God created man in His own image, in the image and likeness of God He created him; male and female He created them.

And God blessed them and said to them, "Be fruitful, multiply, and fill the earth, and subdue it [using all its vast resources in the service of God and man]; and have dominion over the fish of the sea, the birds of the air, and over every living creature that moves upon the earth."

Isaiah 49:15 NLT

Can a mother forget the baby at compassion on the child she has borne? Though she may forget, I will not forget you!

Psalm 33:18 NLT

The LORD watches over those who fear Him, those who rely on His unfailing love.

Psalm 18:6 ESV

In my distress, I called upon the LORD; to my God, I cried for help. From his temple, he heard my voice, and my cry to Him reached His ears.

Jeremiah 29:11 KJV

"For I know the thoughts I think toward you," says the LORD, "thoughts of peace and not of evil, to give you a future and a hope."

Psalm 139:16–17 NIV

Your eyes saw my substance, being yet unformed. And in Your book, they all were written, the days fashioned for me, when as yet there were none of them. How precious also are Your thoughts to me, O God! How great is the sum of them!

Matthew 10:29–31 NKJV

Are not two sparrows sold for a copper coin? And not one of them falls to the ground apart from your Father's will. But the very hairs of your head are all numbered. Do not fear therefore; you are of more value than many sparrows.

ACKNOWLEDGMENTS

First and foremost, I thank God in Heaven, my Heavenly Father, for giving me this assignment and helping me deliver it even when I felt incapable, insecure, and afraid of the outcome. Thank you, Dear LORD, for what I've gained from it and for the outcome, which is solely in your hands.

Thank you, Tarsha Campbell, for walking with me this past year. It reminds me of physical training runs from my army days. When a fellow soldier was struggling to finish the run, one or two of us would run back to them and finish the run with them. Thank you for running with me. My second wind has come.

I am so thankful and indebted to my "First Read Team." You endured the very rough first draft in January 2022, and gave me incredible feedback. You were the first to have a glimpse into what I felt was so important to complete. I trusted the five of you with this work in progress, and now I honor you. Thank you, Kevin and Trudi Clark, Christie Conyers, Charlene Stevens-Jenkins, and Simon Steele.

I thank my love, Nathan Jones, for doing life with me. You have listened to me go on and on about my passions from the time we met—until now, almost 18 years later.

Thank you mom, Audrey Terry, our queen. I thank my incredible circle of family and friends. I started listing names and discovered there's not enough space, and I'm grateful for that.

Last, but certainly not least, I thank you, dear reader. This is for you.

ABOUT THE AUTHOR

DAISY JONES is a woman graced by God's love and divine purpose. She is a retired army lieutenant colonel and life-long learner. She has a bachelor of science in broadcast journalism, as well as master's degrees in human resource management and leadership and management. She is a minister, radio and podcast host, freelance writer, and nonprofit management consultant.

She is graced with a beautiful circle of family and friends.

Other products by Daisy Jones

Finding Strength in Hard Places, Devotional

Church Administration: The Science. The Art. The Gift.

Destiny, 2008 CD

Online
www.conversationswithdaisyjones.com
www.tealirislegacy.com

CONTACT THE AUTHOR

You are welcome to email or write the author with comments about this book. You are also welcome to contact her for bookings. Daisy is available for book club presentations, book signings, and speaking engagements for small group studies, conferences, workshops, retreats, seminars, women's groups, women's ministries, and women's clubs special events, and broadcasts.

Contact information:
Daisy Jones

(912) 318-4346

conversationswithdaisy@gmail.com

Connect with Daisy on social media at:
@convoswithdaisy - FaceBook

@daisyterryjones - FaceBook

@conversationswithdaisyjones - IG

NOTES

www.ingramcontent.com/pod-product-compliance
Lightning Source LLC
LaVergne TN
LVHW010219070526
838199LV00062B/4660